Simon Peter
Sinner and Saint

Simon Peter

Sinner and Saint

by
M. R. DeHaan, M.D.

ZONDERVAN PUBLISHING HOUSE

Simon Peter

Copyright 1954 by
Zondervan Publishing House
Grand Rapids, Michigan

Assigned to the Radio Bible Class 1966

Sixteenth printing 1981
ISBN 0-310-23481-6

Printed in the United States of America

To all God's struggling children, who, like Peter have no confidence in the flesh; who, admit with Paul, "I know that in me, (that is, in my flesh,) dwelleth no good thing"; who seek for victory outside themselves, only in the Lord Jesus Christ,

THIS VOLUME IS PRAYERFULLY DEDICATED

INTRODUCTION

AN exhaustive study of the life of Simon Peter would require many, many volumes. No attempt, therefore, is made in these messages to cover all the details recorded in the gospels, the book of Acts, and Peter's epistles. Rather we have chosen those typical incidents, here and there, in the life of this colorful disciple, which are most characteristic of his personality. In choosing these incidents for study, we have borne in mind two things:

1. We have chosen those incidents which are in our judgment the most important both in doctrine and in practice.

2. We have chosen those on which there is the most difference of opinion and need for clarification.

Many incidents we have been compelled to pass by for lack of space. Such incidents as Peter's walking on the water, the healing of his mother-in-law, his action in causing the disciples to choose Matthias as the twelfth apostle in the book of Acts, his cutting off of Malchus' ear in the Garden, and many others we have been compelled to omit. These would all make interesting studies, to be sure, even as would a study of the two epistles which Simon Peter was permitted to write just before he died. We trust, however, that the fragmentary study of Simon Peter in this volume will stimulate many to continue their own study of this interesting character more fully for themselves. We can assure one and all that such a study will prove a great blessing, as it has been to us as we prepared these messages in this book.

The messages in this volume were specifically prepared for broadcasting purposes over the air, and are reproduced with a minimum of editing and revision. There will, therefore, be some repetition of important truths, but only for the sake of emphasizing those subjects which we deemed of unusual importance.

The study of Peter's life is more than a biographical sketch, for in the life of Peter we find illustrated every important Biblical doctrine, as a glimpse at the table of contents will reveal. In studying the life of Peter we come face to face with the great doctrines of Sin, Salvation, Faith, the Deity of Christ, Justification, Sanctification, the Two Natures, the Christian's Struggle between Flesh and Spirit, the New Birth, the Victorious Life, the Church, the Ordinances, and practically every other great doctrine. These messages, therefore, have a two-fold purpose:

1. Doctrinal Teaching
2. Practical Exhortation

This is the order in the epistles of the New Testament, and the study of Simon Peter lends itself in a most admirable way to this order. We send forth this volume with the prayer that even as the messages were owned of God and blessed when given over the air, they may prove of even greater blessing to multitudes of others as they appear in this more permanent form. We would make the closing admonition of Simon Peter in II Peter 3:18 our own admonition to you, that as a result of these pages you too may:

"Grow in grace, and in the knowledge of our Lord and Saviour Jesus Christ. To him be glory both now and for ever. Amen" (II Peter 3:18)

Grand Rapids, Michigan   M. R. De Haan, M.D.

CONTENTS

Simon Peter

Sinner and Saint

Chapter One

MEET MR. SIMON

Again the next day after John stood, and two of his disciples:

And looking upon Jesus as he walked, he saith, Behold the Lamb of God!

And the two disciples heard him speak, and they followed Jesus . . .

One of the two which heard John speak, and followed him, was Andrew, Simon Peter's brother.

He first findeth his own brother Simon, and saith unto him, We have found the Messias, which is being interpreted, the Christ.

And he brought him to Jesus. And when Jesus beheld him, he said, Thou art Simon the son of Jona: thou shalt be called Cephas, which is by interpretation, A stone.

John 1:35-37; 40-42

IN this account we are introduced for the first time to one of the most exasperating, yet withal one of the most colorful, intriguing and fascinating characters in the entire New Testament: Simon Peter, the great paradox among the disciples. There is none other among all the persons mentioned in the gospels who arouses in our hearts such a conflict of emotions, such extremes of feeling, such a paradox of reactions as this man, Simon Peter.

One moment we admire him for his bold, reckless courage, the next we are tempted to despise him for his silly cowardice. One moment we want to applaud him for his frankness and

11

unaffected confession of his Lord; the next, we want to condemn him for his base denial of the same Lord. One moment he extols the Christ he loved, and the next he denies Him with cursing and swearing. For out of the mouth of this man, Simon Peter, we hear not only the confession, "Thou art the Christ, the son of the living God" but a little later that same mouth belches forth cursing and swearing, as he proclaims with emphatic profanity, that he never knew Him at all. One moment with utter disregard for his own safety, he draws his sword against an army to defend his Lord; an hour later he withers before the leering eyes and sharp tongue of a waitress in the hall of the high priest.

Yet this most exasperating of all the apostles, this inconsistent, wavering, faltering, paradoxical Simon Peter, was destined to become the leader of the apostles; the great Pentecostal preacher; the one to whom Christ delivered The keys of the kingdom; the one who in the end was to glorify God by gladly dying for his Lord; and according to tradition, was crucified head down, because he felt unworthy to be crucified like his Lord.

The Grace of God

Many indeed are the lessons from the life of Peter, and we shall point out some of these in this book. We wish to make it more than a biographical discussion of the record of an intensely interesting person, for in the study of Peter we shall come face to face with practically every great doctrine of the Bible. We shall see an unexcelled revelation of the grace of God in choosing this most unlikely subject to be the leading disciple. We shall come face to face with the doctrine of flesh and spirit, so much misunderstood. We shall see a striking illustration of the two natures in the believer; we shall recognize the doctrine of the two births, as seen in Simon the sinner by his first birth, and Peter the saint by his second birth, resulting in that painful conflict of the two men, the old Simon and the new Peter, the old man and the new. We shall see the two possibilities of the Christian life, mere salvation, and discipleship, the carnal life and the spiritual life, eternal life, and the life abundant.

Only as we look at this man, Simon Peter, not merely as Simon the son of Jona; or as Peter, the son of God, but as "Simon Peter" both saint and sinner, shall we ever be able to explain the seeming inconsistency of Peter's life, and the apparent contradiction of this man's conduct; now blowing hot, now blowing cold; now brave, and the next moment a whimpering coward. Psychologists and psychiatrists, and psycho-analysts would find Peter an exceedingly interesting subject, and his conduct an interesting study, but they would never be able to explain him. They might understand Simon, or be able to explain Peter, but never could they explain SIMON PETER, the saint and the sinner.

THE TWO NATURES

The Bible alone gives the answer to the riddle of Simon Peter. It alone explains how Peter, a saved man, a disciple of Christ, the leader of the apostles, could fall to depths so deep, so low that we associate them only with unbelievers, rejectors of Christ, and the basest of sinners. But our Lord Jesus understood perfectly. He knew the conflict which raged in the heart of Simon Peter; He knew the battle which Peter faced, and was patient, kind, understanding, and always ready to correct, help, restore and forgive his erring child.

May God give us grace to be like Him. Oh, that we might be as kind and tender and helpful to our weak, stumbling, erring, fellow-members of the Body of Christ, the thousands of Simon Peters among us, instead of being so ready to criticize, condemn and excommunicate in our own self-righteousness.

The key to Peter's seeming double personality lay entirely in the fact that Simon Peter all his life remained both Simon and Peter. Peter never got rid of old Simon, but thank God, Simon also never ceased to be new Peter either. Throughout the record his name remains ever "Simon Peter." Sometimes Simon is on top; then again Peter is most in evidence. The key to the enigma of Peter's life is given in the passage with which we began this message. At the first meeting of our Lord and Simon, He says: "Thou art Simon . . . thou shalt be called Peter." In these two names we have the secret of Peter's paradoxical life. His first name was Simon. The Hebrew equivalent is Simeon, the same as Simon in the Greek. This was his name by his first birth, Simon the son of Jonah, for Simon's father's name was Jonah (John).

There came a day, however, when Simon received another name through another birth. We have the record of this in John 1:41. After Andrew had found Jesus, we read:

He (Andrew) first findeth his own brother Simon . . .

And he brought him *to* Jesus. And when Jesus beheld him, he said, Thou art Simon the son of Jona: *thou shalt be* called Cephas, which is by interpretation, A stone (John 1:41-42).

After Andrew had brought Simon *to* Jesus, the Lord promises him a new name, Cephas. It is the Hebrew word for "stone." The Greek equivalent is "Petros" translated as "Peter" in our Bible, and meaning "a stone." For all practical purposes, then, we may take this first meeting of Simon and Jesus as the occasion of Peter's salvation. Simon came *to* Jesus, and coming *to* Him, he was saved. No man can truly come *to* Christ, and not be saved. He Himself has said:

"Him that cometh unto me, I will in no wise cast out."
When, therefore, Simon came *to* Jesus, he was then and there saved. And now take careful notice of this one fact. When Simon was saved, nothing happened at all to the "old" Simon. Salvation does not change the old man, or the old nature. He was still the same Simon. Simon did not become Peter. And so the Lord says to Simon:

"Thou art Simon, son of Jona."

We need to stop here just a moment. Jesus reminds him that he is Simon, son of Jona. Jesus reminds him that by his natural birth he is the son of a man, the son of John, and he received his father's nature, sinful, corrupt, depraved, blind, helpless, condemned, with a wicked heart, which God describes as "Deceitful above all things, and desperately wicked."

This old, sinful heart is Simon's heart, Simon's nature by his first birth, which cannot be changed, corrected, altered, fixed up or improved, but must be constantly fought against, opposed, put down, defeated, starved, and ultimately destroyed. And so Jesus addresses him as "Simon son of Jona." Oh, how Peter needed that reminder. How often afterwards he must have recalled how Jesus first addressed him as "Simon, son of Jona." Years afterward, Simon proved that he was still there, as he blunders and stumbles and falls and even denies his Lord.

Simon and Peter

And now we come to Cephas (Peter). Notice again Jesus' words: "Thou art Simon the son of Jona: thou shalt be called Cephas, which is by interpretation, A stone." John 1:42

Here our Lord Jesus introduces the new man. Simon is promised a new name, Cephas. It is not until Peter had publicly confessed Christ in Matthew 16 that he is actually called Peter. In our present passage we read: "Thou *shalt be called* Cephas." It is a promise, but not until his public declaration of faith in Matthew 16 do we read:

"Thou Art Peter"

We repeat, however, and shall repeat over and over again, Simon did not become Peter. Peter was not only a new name, but a new man, *not* a changed Simon, not a converted Simon, but a new Peter, entirely. Notice carefully, therefore, that when Jesus said, "Thou art Peter," He did not drop or replace the name Simon, but from now on he is to be Simon Peter. How emphatically the Lord asserts this great truth. When the time for Peter's great confession came in Matthew 16, and Peter had confessed the Lord, Jesus said:

"Blessed art thou, Simon Bar-jona: (son of John) for flesh and blood hath not revealed it unto thee, but my Father which is in heaven.

And I say also unto thee, That thou art Peter (a stone) . . ." (Matthew 16:17-18)

Do you see how Jesus reminds him that he is still Simon, son of John, and this new revelation concerning Jesus as the Christ resulting in Peter's confession, was a super-natural revelation from heaven. It was not something Simon had figured out or reasoned out. Ah, no! Flesh and blood had not revealed it unto him. The old nature had nothing to do with this confession. It was a supernatural gift of God, for says Christ:

"Flesh and blood hath not revealed it unto thee, *but my Father which is in Heaven*" (Matthew 16:18).

By your first birth, Simon, you are the son of your father, John, flesh and blood, blinded by depravity, and you could never come to me by yourself. This knowledge of Me, this confession, is the voice of the new nature, the gift of My Father in heaven. By your first birth you were flesh and blood, a son of Adam. Now by faith in Me, you have become a Son of God, a child of My Father, and while your name is still Simon, your new name is now Peter, and now you are two men, Simon, the Sinner, and Peter, the Saint. Now you have two natures, the old and the new. And now, Simon Peter, the battle is on, and there can be no compromise, no armistice, no retreat, no cease-fire, until the final victory of Peter over Simon has been accomplished. The flesh will never become spirit, but must be overcome by the spirit.

Christian, do you recognize your own picture in all this? Are you too having a struggle? Do you too long to live the life of victory over the flesh, and yearn for true holiness? Then continue to study with us the life of Simon Peter, honestly recognizing the presence of the old man within you, instead of denying it. Never forget, he is there. Never ignore his presence. If you are not aware of his presence, he is only "playing possum." He has just gone underground. You can only overcome him by being constantly on the alert, and conscious of his presence. Press the battle, even unto the end. This victory only comes by a sincere and careful study of the Word, a life of prayer, honest confession of our sin, daily witnessing for Him, and keeping the flesh always on the defensive, until that day when He shall present us with all the saints, ". . . a glorious church, not having spot, or wrinkle, or any such thing; but that it should be holy and without blemish" (Ephesians 5:27).

Chapter Two

PETER AND THE NEW BIRTH

One of the two which heard John speak, and followed him, was Andrew, Simon Peter's brother.

He first findeth his own brother Simon, and saith unto him, We have found the Messias, which is, being interpreted, the Christ.

And he brought him to Jesus.   John 1:40-42

THIS is our introduction to Simon Peter, and Simon Peter's introduction to our Lord. Of all the characters in the gospels, none are as interesting and provoking as the man we know as Simon Peter, the disciple of our Lord. None could rise to such heights of spiritual enthusiasm and loyalty; none could fall to such depths of weakness and depravity and denial of the Master. Simon Peter is a study in conflicts and contrasts.

One moment he cries, "Though all forsake thee, I never shall. I will die for thee," and a moment later he is scared to death by a waitress and denies that same Lord with cursing and swearing. It is quite difficult to believe that this can be the same individual, Peter the believer, and at the same time, Simon, the denier. Simon Peter brings us face to face with the two natures in the believer—the flesh and the spirit; the old man and the new man; the Adamic nature and the Divine nature.

The names by which this disciple of Christ is known suggest this great truth of the two natures in the believer, so little understood by most Christians. He is most frequently known, not as Simon, not as Peter, but rather as Simon Peter — Simon the son of John and Peter the son of God.

These two names suggest to us two births, the natural and the spiritual. By his first birth he was Simon; by his second birth he became Peter. When he became Peter he did not cease to be Simon, however. When a person is born anew, the old is not improved or reformed or fixed up. No indeed, Simon does not become Peter, but God creates a brand new nature, a new man by the new birth, and places it alongside the old, so that now he is not only Simon, but also Peter, and, therefore, "Simon Peter."

THE OLD AND THE NEW

Our first introduction to Simon is in John 1:41. Here Andrew, having found Jesus, first brings his brother.

"He first findeth his own brother Simon . . ."

Notice carefully that Andrew found Simon—not Peter. Simon meets Jesus as Simon, the sinner, and only after meeting Him does he become Peter, the saint. Simon can only become Peter after he has come to the Lord Jesus. When he comes, he becomes a new creation. In Matthew 16:15, Jesus asked His disciples what men said concerning Him, and they gave various answers. Some said He was John the Baptist, others Elias, others Jeremiah, others one of the prophets. Then to the question, "Whom say ye that I am?" Simon Peter speaks up and says: "Thou art the Christ, the Son of the living God" (Matthew 16:16).

Then it is that Jesus answers and says unto him: "Blessed art thou, Simon son of John."

That was Peter's first name by his first birth—Simon, born

of John, his natural father. Now notice the following verse:

"And I say also unto thee, That thou art Peter, and upon this rock I will build my church" (Matthew 16:18).

It is upon the occasion of his confession of Christ that he receives the new name, "Peter," meaning "a stone." And from now on he is not only Simon, not only Peter, but Simon Peter, and remains so until the time of his death. He is now two men, the old and the new, the flesh and the spirit, and the battle is on. Sometimes old Simon flashes forth, and then again Peter is in the supremacy. How clearly the conflict of the two natures is seen in this man Peter, the conflict which Paul describes when he says:

"For the flesh lusteth against the Spirit, and the Spirit against the flesh: and these are contrary the one to the other: so that ye cannot do the things that ye would" (Galatians 5:17).

Or again,

"For I know that in me (that is, in my flesh) dwelleth no good thing" (Romans 7:18).

Christian Victory

True spiritual victory depends upon recognizing the old nature within us at all times. To ignore him, to deny his existence, is to let the Trojan horse enter the citadel of our hearts. It can only result in tragedy and defeat sooner or later. True victory comes only by recognizing the enemy, and preparing to overcome him. Simon Peter, until his dying day, recognized the old flesh within him, and even in his last epistle he introduces himself as Simon Peter (II Peter 1:1).

Simon Peter

Simon Peter is the picture of every born-again believer. By nature we are all sinners; by our first birth we are of the flesh, lost and undone, depraved and under condemnation. When, like Simon, we come to Jesus, He saves us, and we receive a brand new nature—the Peter nature—the stone. But right here many err, for they now suppose that the old nature is either eradicated, improved, changed, or altered in some way, born over or corrected. But the Bible teaches no such thing.

JESUS AND NICODEMUS

Nowhere is it better illustrated than in the case of Nicodemus, Jesus tells this fine, upstanding, moral, upright, religious man:

"Except a man be born again, he cannot see the kingdom of God" (John 3:3).

Now the word, "again" in this verse is *anothen*, and means "from above." So what Jesus actually says is:

"Except a man be born from above, he cannot see the kingdom of God."

But Nicodemus missed the point entirely. He imagined that this new birth was a "rebirth" of the old man. He imagined that to be born "again" meant for the old man to be born all over again in the natural way, and so he replies to our Saviour:

"How can a man be born when he is old? can he enter the second time into his mother's womb, and be born?" (John 3:4)

He imagined that the new birth meant a rebirth of the same old man. But says Jesus, it is nothing of the kind, and He explains it in verse 5,

"Except a man be born of water and of the Spirit, he cannot enter into the kingdom of God" (John 3:5).

To be born again of the flesh the second time would only result in a repetition of the first natural birth. If this first natural birth could be repeated ten thousand times, it would still do absolutely no good. It would still result in the same kind of a man and the same kind of a nature. A man must be born from above. This is quite a different birth from the first birth. The first was by flesh and blood; this one is by water (the Word of God) and the Spirit. Now notice what follows in this chapter:

"That which is born of the flesh is flesh; and that which is born of the Spirit is spirit" (John 3:6).

What Jesus means to say is that we need, not a rebirth of the old man, but a new birth of the Spirit. Flesh is flesh, and always remains flesh, and can never be anything else. Spirit is Spirit, and always remains Spirit, and can never be anything else. You cannot change flesh into Spirit, or Spirit into flesh, for the two will never mix. They are distinct, they are forever separate, there can be no peace, no armistice, no cease-fire, until the old is completely overcome and done away with. It is war to the bitter end.

Surely we need not argue the point of the believer's conflict in view of these two natures. We see it in the life of Jacob; in the life of David; in the life of Peter; and in the life of Paul as he cries out in Romans 7:

"I find then a law, that, when I would do good, evil is present with me.

For I delight in the law of God after the inward man:

But I see another law in my members, warring against the law of my mind, and bringing me into captivity to the law of sin which is in my members.

O wretched man that I am! who shall deliver me from the body of this death?" (Romans 7:21-24)

This is not only Paul's experience, but it is Simon Peter all over again. It is Simon the old, against Peter the new, and Peter the new against Simon the old. This was true also of

Paul, even until the end of his life. He recognized the conflict which raged within him, and claimed the victory only through the Lord Jesus Christ. He admitted that he did not have the power within his old nature to overcome sin, but only as he was willing to yield his all to Christ was there any possibility of victory at all.

To bring this whole discussion closer home, for we do want to make these things intensely practical, we ask the question, "Is there a believer who is not conscious of these two natures within him?" We may have the victory, and live above the old to be sure and yet always be conscious that there is within us, in our flesh, no good thing.

The Old Nature Still With Us

In a moment of carelessness, in a moment of weakness, in a moment when we become over-confident, we are all too prone to fall and be bitterly and painfully reminded that the old nature is still within us. The moment of greatest danger in the Christian's life is when he reaches that stage where he believes he has gained the victory, and becomes careless. When we feel the most secure, we are in the greatest danger, and need to be reminded again and again not to have any confidence in the flesh.

Ah, do you not feel within your own heart the need for constant dependence upon the grace of God, through prayer and by the Word and by communion and by confession, and keeping busy in His work. Is there a moment of the day when we need not to look to Him for victory? It has been the testimony of the Godliest people in all ages, that they have had a deep sense of their own weakness and their own guilt and their own failure, which drove them to an utter dependence on God for victory, and God alone. And so Paul does cry out:

"O wretched man that I am! who shall deliver me from
the body of this death?" (Romans 7:24)

It was only when Paul looked outside of himself entirely,
and was willing to look to Christ, that the answer follows; and
he cries out in victory in verse 25:

"I thank God through Jesus Christ our Lord" (Romans
7:25).

We see the two natures and the Christian conflict, also
in the life of Peter, and we remind you, that while the battle
will continue as long as these two are present within us, it is
not necessary to suffer defeat. We have within us One who is
always, every moment of the day, capable of giving victory
over the old, helping us to live a life pleasing to God.

Gain the Victory

Here are four important steps which I believe are absolutely
necessary and indispensable in gaining the victory God wants
us to have. They are:

1. Recognize our own sinfulness, and never fall into the
error of supposing the enemy, even though he may not be
apparent, has forsaken us. Sometimes the enemy goes under
ground, and is submerged, but those are the very moments
when we need to be especially on guard. The first essential,
therefore, is always to recognize the presence within us of the
old nature, the flesh. This is essential. Unless this is recognized, everything else must fail.

2. Second, we must seek His grace in forgiveness when
we do err. If when we stumble and fall, as all God's people
are prone to do, we are not to despair and believe that He
has cast us off again, but to remember that He knew all about
this before He saved us, and is waiting even now to cleanse us
and make us wholly clean. He has given us the promise:

"If we confess our sins, he is faithful and just to forgive us our sins, and to cleanse us from all unrighteousness" (I John 1:9).

This is God's provision for the believer when and if he falls
(he should not, but he too often does.)

3. Appropriate the power of God by faith in His promises,
and in the power of prayer. By keeping in constant touch with
Him, through a life of prayer, we shall be in constant communication with the only source of victory and power. A life
without prayer is a life of defeat.

4. Obey His Word in regard to practical holiness. No
Christian can have the victory without being saturated with
the Word of God. If there is one cause for the all-too-frequent
defeat of Christians, it is because they have not been feeding
upon the Word of God.

So in conclusion we would like to repeat this. Never,
never ignore the presence of the enemy. Seek to know all
about him. Receive God's grace and strength when momentarily you have been defeated. Rely upon Him by faith
and prayer, and saturate yourself with the Word of God.
Claim the promises, and keep busy for Him.

Chapter Three

PETER AND THE TWO NATURES

*That which is born of the flesh is flesh; and that which
is born of the Spirit is spirit.*
Marvel not that I said unto thee, Ye must be born again,

John 3:6-7

SOMEONE has said, "All men who have been born only
once, will have to die twice, spiritually and physically. However, all who have been born twice will die only once, physically but never spiritually, and those who should live till
the Lord comes will never die." By our first birth we are children of wrath, totally depraved, dead in trespasses and sins.
This nature we receive at our natural birth is the nature of
father Adam, incorrigibly corrupt, unable to do a single thing
to please God.

By our second birth we receive a new nature, the nature
of God, a divine nature which can never perish, never sin,
never die. It is called the divine nature (II Peter 1:4). The
believer, therefore, has two natures, the old and the new,
the human and the divine, the sinful and the sinless, the dead
and the living. But we must never forget when the sinner by
the grace of God receives the new nature in the new birth,
nothing happens to the old. We make bold to repeat this over
and over again. The new birth is a *new* birth, not a *rebirth*.
The two are totally distinct and separate, and will ever remain
so. Sin made such absolute ruin of the Adamic nature that
even God does not bother to try and repair, improve or

26

change it, but instead offers his own nature, the divine life of Himself, to all who will believe.

BASIC ERROR

Again we point out that nowhere is this better illustrated than in the life of Simon Peter. We remind you again, Simon Peter was two men, Simon and Peter. Sometimes Simon has the upper hand, and then again Peter is the Master. And this struggle lasted until the day of Simon Peter's death. I am sure that a few illustrations from his life will emphasize this great and imperative truth. In Matthew 16 we first hear Peter, and then Simon speaking. Listen first to Peter:

"When Jesus came into the coasts of Caesarea Philippi, he asked his disciples, saying, Whom do men say that I the Son of man am?

And they said, Some say that thou art John the Baptist: some, Elias; and others, Jeremias, or one of the prophets.

He saith unto them, But whom say ye that I am?

And *Simon Peter* answered and said, Thou art the Christ, the Son of the living God" (Matthew 16:13-16).

That was the "Peter" part of Simon Peter speaking. It was the voice of the new nature, and Jesus clinches it in the next verse by these words:

"And Jesus answered and said unto him, Blessed art thou, Simon Bar-jona: for flesh and blood hath not revealed it unto thee, but my Father which is in heaven" (Matthew 16:17).

Jesus asserts that this confession was not the revelation of "flesh and blood," (the Bible term for the Adamic nature) but the divine revelation of the Spirit of God.

SUDDEN CHANGE

Notice how quickly the old Simon nature could again assert itself, after this wonderful confession of the Lord

Jesus. It is only a moment after Jesus had said to him, "Thou art Peter, and upon this rock I will build my church," that He told them some very unwelcome news, to prepare their hearts for His passion and death.

"From that time forth began Jesus to shew unto his disciples, how that he must go unto Jerusalem, and suffer many things of the elders and chief priests and scribes, and be killed, and be raised again the third day" (Matthew 16:21).

Our Lord now begins to prepare the hearts of His disciples for the greatest disappointment of their lives. They had expected, that Messiah, when He came would set up the Kingdom, deliver Israel, and bring in the Messianic reign of peace and righteousness, foretold by all the prophets of old. It was largely in this expectation of His Kingdom that they had left all, and followed Him. Now He announces apparent defeat, instead of anticipated victory; a crown of thorns instead of a diadem; a Cross instead of a throne. This was hard on the flesh, and immediately Simon answers, and we read this from the lips of the same man who only a moment before had made the great confession, "Thou art the Christ."

"Then Peter took him, and began to rebuke him, saying, Be it far from thee, Lord: this shall not be unto thee" (Matthew 16:22).

REBUKING THE LORD

How incredible and contradictory all of this becomes, unless we recognize the fact of the two natures in the believer, the old man, Simon, and the new man, Peter. Here is Peter permitting the flesh to *rebuke* his Lord. Think of it! The disciple rebuking his Master! How inconsistent to call Him Lord, and then to rebuke and contradict Him. But Jesus recognized the voice of the flesh as being instigated by the devil himself, and so we read that difficult verse, so often misunderstood:

"But he (Jesus) turned, and said unto Peter, Get thee behind me, Satan: thou art an offence unto me: for thou savourest not the things that be of God, but those that be of men" (Matthew 16:23).

Now this strange answer of Jesus, in turning to Peter and rebuking the devil, is a marvelous picture of the indescribable, unfathomable love and grace of the Saviour. The Lord understood the struggle within Simon Peter's heart, the two voices that battled for expression, the voice of the Spirit, and the voice of the flesh; the voice of God, and the voice of Satan. And so our Lord turns to Peter and says:

"Get thee behind me, Satan."

We might have expected our Lord to disown Peter entirely. But Jesus does nothing of the kind. He simply reminds Peter that the flesh is still with him, and in a moment of overconfidence, he was able to fall. Peter, do you know what you have said? Do you realize that it was the devil who prompted you to rebuke Me? Peter should have rebuked the devil himself, and told him to "Get thee behind me." But Simon must learn the great lesson — have no confidence in the flesh, and confess, as all believers must confess, that "in me, that is in my flesh, there dwelleth no good thing."

BECOMES A DISCIPLE

Then there follows Jesus' great teaching on discipleship. In the next verse we read:

"Then said Jesus unto his disciples, If any man will come after me, let him deny himself, and take up his cross, and follow me.

For whosoever will save his life shall lose it: and whosoever will lose his life for my sake shall find it" (Matthew 16:24-25).

Peter needed this lesson. He was still a babe in the faith, he still had a long, long way to go. His was not to be a "once-for-all" experience of eradication, an immediate sanctification, one single step to sinless perfection, but it was to be a daily growth in grace and power as a result of following the Lord and becoming a "disciple," a learner, till at last the victory would be his. Peter knew that Bible sanctification was a daily experience, a constant growth. Peter knew better than to be carried away by the deception, that we can get rid of the flesh and the old nature. He knew better than to be beguiled by the subtle error of eradication of the old man.

PETER'S LAST WORDS

Simon Peter clinches all this in no uncertain way. When he comes to the very end of his life and has only a few days to live, he bears testimony to this fact. He had evidently been condemned to die for his Lord, and knew that it was to be soon. We know this, of course, from II Peter 1:14. Peter's last words before he dies are:

"Knowing that shortly I must put off this my tabernacle, even as our Lord Jesus Christ hath shewed me." (II Peter 1:14).

Peter knew this was his last word to us before he died. Notice how this last letter begins and ends. In verse 1 we read:

"Simon Peter."

What a significant opening for his last epistle — *Simon Peter*. It was not merely Peter, as it was in the first epistle. Peter did not boast that "old" Simon was finally gone, eradicated, root and branch. Ah, no! Peter knew better than that. It had been a long, long struggle, and now, as he sees complete and permanent and eternal victory within his grasp he admits that the flesh is still with him. And to clinch it once for all, notice how the last epistle of Peter ends. The last verse of the last chapter of Peter's last message is:

"But grow in grace, and in the knowledge of our Lord and Saviour Jesus Christ. To him be glory both now and for ever. Amen" (II Peter 3:18).

This is Simon Peter's last message to us. Never relax the struggle until we meet our Lord and our Captain face to face.

We want to make these messages practical to all, and help you to face the realities of your Christian experiences as they are, not only as you would like to have them be. And so we ask the question again, Are you troubled at the constant battle you have to face? So many are. Many people seem to have an unusual struggle as they pass through this life, as our good friend, Peter, also had. Some of them even doubt their salvation, and wonder whether victory is possible. It is hard for them to understand that it is *not* sin to be tempted, but it *is* sin to yield. It is not a sin to have a battle with the flesh, but it is a sin to submit to the flesh. Are you conscious of the presence within you of that which would draw you constantly away from God? Then remember your only hope is:

1. Recognize the deceitfulness of the flesh, and

2. That you have within you also the new nature with the power to make you more than conquerors through Him that loved us.

It is no use ignoring this old man, no use denying it. Our only hope when we fall is to confess and return to the Lord and recognize the fact that the Christian life is a development, a growth in grace. Just as a child is born an infant and needs to be trained and educated before it reaches maturity, so too the Christian life begins in weakness and needs to be fed and nourished and exercised and trained so that we may be able to meet the battles of life which lie ahead.

In closing this portion of our study, therefore, let me again give a few rules for victory.

1. Recognize the presence of the flesh. This is the first essential, and without it you cannot go on any farther.

2. Recognize that within, you also have the divine nature which, if you will recognize and yield to, can give you daily victory over the flesh, the world and the devil.

3. Without prayer, constant communication with Headquarters, victory is always impossible.

4. Remember that we have written orders given by the Captain of our salvation, and to neglect our Bibles must always end in defeat.

Here is a closing admonition. When in the heat of the battle you do fall, and you do fail, and you suffer defeat, do not despair, but remember that our Captain has also made provision for this, and told us:

> "My little children, these things write I unto you, that ye sin not. And if any man sin, we have an advocate with the Father, Jesus Christ the righteous:

> And he is the propitiation for our sins: and not for ours only, but also for the sins of the whole world" (I John 2:1-2).

Have you been defeated? Then will you make this moment the time when you will turn to Him and receive His cleansing, and go forth stronger because of the experience you have had, putting you on guard as you have never been on guard before?

Chapter Four

CHRISTIAN VICTORY

Jesus answered, Verily verily, I say unto thee, Except a man be born of water and of the Spirit, he cannot enter into the kingdom of God.

John 3:5

Being born again, not of corruptible seed, but of incorruptible, by the word of God, which liveth and abideth for ever. For all flesh is as grass, and all the glory of man as the flower of grass. The grass withereth, and the flower thereof falleth away:

But the word of the Lord endureth for ever, And this is the word which by the gospel is preached unto you.

I Peter 1:23-25

THE Lord Jesus Christ said, "Except a man be born again, he cannot see the kingdom of God." (John 3:3) By his first birth every human being is dead in trespasses and sins, totally corrupt, unable to please God or save himself. Something, therefore, must be done or man is eternally lost. Since man himself is utterly helpless to save himself, God must find a way to save mankind. But sin must first be dealt with, and this was done by Jesus Christ, who bare our sins in His own Body on the Tree. Jesus paid for our sins, provided a righteousness for sinners, and imparts this salvation in the new birth.

33

Must Be Born Again

Jesus said, *"Ye must* be born again." It is not only desirable, but imperative. John tells us how this new life is received. It is born:

". . . not of blood, nor of the will of the flesh, nor of the will of man, but of God" (John 1:13).

It is the divine life, the God-life, which in the new birth is imparted to the believer. Peter says in II Peter 1:4,

"Whereby are given unto us exceeding great and precious promises: that by these ye might be partakers of the *divine* nature . . ."

The new birth is not a re-birth. It is not being "born again." It would be of little use to be born over again from human parents. If a man could be born over a thousand times, it would still leave him a poor, helpless, lost sinner with Adam's fallen, depraved nature within him. And that is exactly what troubled Nicodemus, after Jesus had said to him:

"Verily, verily, I say unto thee, Except a man be born again, he cannot see the kingdom of God" (John 3:3).

Nicodemus recognized not only how incongruous this was, but how hopeless, and so he asks the logical question:

"How can a man be born when he is old? can he enter the second time into his mother's womb, and be born?" (John 3:4)

Now that was a good question. What good, he seems to say, will it do if we could reverse the processes of life, and grow younger instead of older, until we were babies again, and go back into our mother's womb, and start all over again from the moment of our conception? What good would it do after all? The result would be just another little sinner, just as we were born the first time. Yes, if this were done ten thousand times, it would still be no different.

THE NEW BIRTH

Now this was the problem Nicodemus faced. He realized that it must be something more than a re-birth, something more than a repetition of the first birth, and so Jesus hastens to explain, and seems to say to this Pharisee, "You don't understand, Nicodemus. I'm not talking about a second birth of the old man, but a new creation, a new man, a new nature, totally distinct and separate from the first." Our Lord explains it in verse 5:

"Verily, verily, I say unto thee, Except a man be born of water and of the Spirit, he cannot enter into the kingdom of God."

"That which is born of the flesh is flesh . . ." (John 3:6a).

It can never, never be anything else, than just flesh, sinful, corrupt, condemned flesh. Religion may try to fix up the flesh, to improve it, to train it. It may seek by a social gospel, reformation and education, by ordinance and ritual, good works and legalism, church membership and restraint, to bring about that which God Himself would not even attempt to do, but it must fail. Man begins with the false, unscriptural assumption of the innate goodness of man. Modern religion tells us there is some good in even the worst; that all of us have a spark of the divine life, and all we need is to encourage, feed, educate, train and fan this little flame of goodness, and it will finally blaze forth in all the light of virtue and salvation by good works and religion.

DENIAL OF THE NEW BIRTH

This philosophy of man is a direct denial of the need of the new birth, and the words of Christ in regard to regeneration. It makes the new birth unnecessary when we substitute church membership, baptism, confirmation and good works for regeneration. But Jesus says to all of this, *No! Ye must* be born again! The man to whom He said it had all of these things — religion, morals, good works, reputation; in short, Nicodemus had everything, but he still needed to be born again.

This new birth then is a completely new creation, wholly apart and distinct from the old. When a person, therefore, is born anew, God places this new nature within him, alongside the old, together with the old man in the believer. The new nature is not a changed, reformed, or regenerated "old" nature, nor does it take the place of the old, but is placed alongside the old, and so every new man becomes two men. Paul says in II Corinthians 5:17,

> "Therefore if any man be in Christ, he is a new creature: old things are passed away: behold, all things are become new."

This is probably the most frequently quoted verse by young converts, but it is seldom understood by those who quote it, well meaning as they may be. This verse applies *only* to the new man. It certainly does not mean that the things of the "old man" are passed away, and all things about a saved person have become new. He still has his temptations, and faults, his weaknesses, physical and spiritual, and is prone to sin, and too frequently does. The saddest thing in life is to see those who claim the old man is gone, root and branch, and completely eradicated, falling by the wayside, and in their false self-confidence slip into the very sins of the flesh which they claim was gone. Yes, the believer is a new creation, but the old is still there, for

"That which is born of the flesh is flesh; and that which is born of the Spirit is spirit" (John 3:6).

This is exactly why there is the struggle in the Christian's life, if we are willing to be honest with ourselves. The flesh is prone to sin; the new nature cannot sin. In the believer there are these two forces pulling in opposite directions, the flesh dragging down, the spirit pulling up. Simon Peter knew this all too well when he cried:

"Depart from me; for I am a sinful man, O Lord" (Luke 5:8).

And our Lord Jesus too recognized it in Simon Peter when He said to Peter:

"Get thee behind me, Satan: thou art an offence unto me: for thou savourest not the things that be of God, but those that be of men" (Matthew 16:23).

Paul the apostle did not deny this when thirty years after he had been saved, he confesses in Galatians 5:16,

"This I say then, Walk in the Spirit, and ye shall not fulfil the lust of the flesh."

Of what purpose, we ask, is this warning and admonition to guard against fulfilling the lusts of the flesh, if the flesh is not present anymore? Why all the warnings to the believer to be on guard, if there is no enemy left to guard against? We need to return once again to Paul's confession in Romans 7:

"For I know that in me (that is, in my flesh,) dwelleth no good thing: for to will is present with me; but how to perform that which is good I find not" (Romans 7:18).

The Apostle Paul with whom we cannot compare ourselves, recognizes that in himself, in his own strength, in the flesh, he is utterly helpless, and honestly confesses:

"For the good that I would I do not: but the evil which I would not, that I do" (Romans 7:19).

Remember this is Paul the Apostle speaking. The good the new man wants to do is opposed constantly by the evil, the old nature, every step along the way. The struggle is between the new and the old, and so he continues in verse 20 of Romans 7:

> "Now if I do that I would not, it is no more I that do it, but sin that dwelleth in me."

Paul wrote this thirty years after he had been saved, and had become a new creation in Christ. He still realized his danger, he knew his need of help outside of himself, and he made no claim or boast of having gotten rid of the old man, once and for all.

Paul realized the hopelessness of battling in his own strength, and turned it all over to the Lord Jesus Christ for victory. But even though he claimed the victory he still remained conscious that the battle would go on until the end, for after his cry of confidence, "I thank God through Jesus Christ our Lord," he still continues:

> "So then with the mind I myself serve the law of God; but with the flesh the law of sin" (Romans 7:25).

Yes, indeed, says Paul, even though I have victory, I still realize that in me, that is in my flesh, there dwelleth no good thing. Victory does not imply that the flesh has been done away with or eradicated, and we still have no confidence in the flesh, and the older it becomes the more rotten it seems to be.

No Condemnation

Now go into the next verse with Paul. There should, of course, never have been any break between chapter seven and chapter eight of Romans. We should go right on from the last verse in Romans 7 into the first verse of Romans 8, where we read:

"There is therefore now no condemnation to them which are in Christ Jesus, who walk not after the flesh, but after the Spirit."

To say that Romans 7 is the experience of Paul before he was sanctified, and Romans 8 is his experience after his second blessing is to violate every rule of Scripture interpretation and is without any Scriptural basis whatsoever. Thirty years after Paul had been saved, he still does not dare to make the claim many young and uninstructed, and ignorant converts make only a few days after they have come to the Lord Jesus. Paul knew himself too well to make any such idle claims. By looking at the passage in Romans 7 you will notice that Paul is not speaking in the past tense, but in the present. He says:

"I know that in me (that is, in my flesh,) dwelleth no good thing" (Romans 7:18).

There are those who tell us Romans 7 was the experience of Paul before he had had a second definite work of grace, and the old man had been completely eradicated, and Romans 8 tells us of the victory which he had after this experience had been accomplished. However, we fail to find anything to support this interpretation in the entire Bible. It is a man of straw made for the occasion in order to explain away this difficult passage. Let me, therefore, remind you that the seventh chapter of Romans, written thirty years after Paul had been saved, is written in the *present tense*. He acknowledges his own utter unworthiness, and turns the struggle over to Christ, and then comes the shout of assurance. In spite of his struggle, in spite of his own utter unworthiness, he rejoices that:

"There is therefore now no condemnation to them which are in Christ Jesus . . ." (Romans 8:1).

To place any other interpretation upon this passage is to violate the Scriptures.

It Is All of Grace

No condemnation, says Paul, in spite of the fact that the old nature is still there, in spite of the fact that we come short each day. No condemnation, for it is all of grace. Even though Paul stumbles and falls, yet, no condemnation! He has a place to go for cleansing, for power to overcome, a place where he can receive the strength to overcome and gain the victory. And this fact, that the Lord stands ever ready to help, forgive and to cleanse, becomes the impelling motive of Paul in his striving for holiness and service.

Personal Admonition

Believer, are you conscious of a daily struggle within you? It is one of the signs of life, and you ought to thank God for the consciousness, and realize also that there is victory and deliverance as we shall point out in the coming messages. Do not make the fatal mistake of closing your eyes to the enemy, to your own flesh and your own weakness, lest you be overcome in a moment of self-confidence and bring disgrace upon the cause of the Lord Jesus Christ. Only as we stop boasting, only as we abandon all confidence in ourselves, and turn it over entirely to the God of all grace, and plead the blood of the Lord Jesus Christ, can we know real triumph over the enemy. This does not mean the enemy is gone, but that we have gained the victory over the enemy. May God help us to understand ourselves in the light of the Word of God.

Chapter Five

PETER, THE FISHERMAN

*And it came to pass, that, as the people pressed upon him
to hear the word of God, he stood by the lake of Gen-
nesaret,*

*And saw two ships standing by the lake: but the fisher-
men were gone out of them, and were washing their
nets.*

*And he entered into one of the ships, which was Simon's,
and prayed him that he would thrust out a little from the
land. And he sat down, and taught the people out of the
ship.*

*Now when he had left speaking, he said unto Simon,
Launch out into the deep, and let down your nets for a
draught.*

*And Simon answering said unto him, Master, we have
toiled all the night, and have taken nothing: nevertheless
at thy word I will let down the net.*

*And when they had this done, they inclosed a great multi-
tude of fishes: and their net brake.*

Luke 5:1-6

THIS second call of the apostle Peter is apparently the same
incident which is recorded in the first chapter of the gospel
according to Mark. We have already seen how Simon had
met Jesus Christ prior to the incident in this chapter, and
had come to Him as his Saviour, but then had gone about

his business again as if nothing had happened. Peter had continued his fishing career, as usual, and there seems to have been no outward change in his life. However, on this particular morning Peter and his fellows, disgusted and weary, had returned from an all night fishing trip without a single fish. They were washing their nets when Jesus interrupted them, and commandeered Simon's ship to act as a sort of a pulpit from which to teach the great multitudes which had come to listen, though it was still early in the day.

After the sermon Jesus orders Simon to pull away from the shore, and to let down the nets. But Simon objects strenuously, and reminds the Lord that it is of no use, for they had fished all night without catching a single fish. But our Lord had something quite different in mind than a net full of ordinary fish. Simon was to learn a new lesson, for which he was now ready, the great lesson of discipleship.

SIMON! SIMON! SIMON!

This great lesson is immediately suggested by the repeated use of the name, "Simon" without the usual surname, "Peter" in this passage. Close study of this passage, if you will underscore each time the name "Simon" occurs, will indicate what we mean. First we are told in verse 3, that Jesus entered into "Simon's" boat (not Simon Peter's). In the next verse Jesus says to "Simon" (not Peter):

"Launch out into the deep."

Again in verse 5 we read:

"And Simon (again not Peter) answering said unto him, Master, we have toiled all the night, and have taken nothing."

It is not until verse 8 where he falls down at Jesus' feet that the full name, "Simon Peter," is used. This is significant indeed. We believe every word in this record was carefully chosen by the Holy Spirit. Dr. Luke is giving it to us just as he received it. There must be some design, some specific purpose in the careful use of the name, Simon, over and over again without the usual surname, Peter.

The reason becomes evident when we remember that "Simon" was the name his natural father, John, had given Peter. Simon represents the old man of the flesh, by his first birth. Simon had come to Christ and become Peter, but in our Scripture we see little evidence of the "Peter," for it is all Simon, all flesh. It is "Simon" from beginning to end. It was Simon who had gone back to his fishing boats; it was Simon who had toiled all night in his own strength. It was into Simon's boat that Jesus chose to enter, to set the stage for the much-needed lesson Simon was about to learn. It was to Simon that Jesus said, "Launch out into the deep, and let down your nets for a draught."

Here is Simon's fleshly answer, and remember it is *Simon* speaking, and not Peter. He asks in essence, "Let down the nets, after we have just finished washing them? It's no use, Lord. I am an old experienced fisherman, and I assure you it will do no good. We have toiled all night and caught nothing. It's no use. If we couldn't catch them during the night, it certainly is a waste of energy to try it in broad day light. We have just finished washing our nets, and now you want us to again soil our nets, and for no good purpose?"

This was the reasoning of Simon, the man of the flesh, the old man who disputed the very words of the One who made the sea and the fish. The flesh is not of faith, and Simon had no faith in his Master's advice. He walked by sight and reason, and not by faith. What a lesson Simon had to learn! For while he insisted it was no use to let down the nets, he protestingly adds, and this is very interesting:

"Nevertheless at thy word I will let down the net"
(Luke 5:5).

This was not an act of obedience, as may appear on the
surface, but an act of absolute unbelief. Simon seems to say,
"I know it will do no good, but just to prove, Lord, how
mistaken You are, I will let down just *one* net." Our Lord
had said to Simon:

Let Down the Nets

Not only one, but all of them, for you will need them, every
one of them. The word is plural, "nets." But Simon says,
"That's foolish, Lord. One net is going to be enough to prove
how wrong you are. There certainly is no use letting down
more than one. There simply are no fish over there, but I
will let down the net, one net, to prove it." This was the
reasoning of Simon after the flesh.

Then came the surprise, for now the multitude of fish was
so great that the net brake. The net was ruined because
Simon had caught in one net the fish that should have been
caught in many nets. How much better if he had only trusted
the Lord in the first place.

In this connection we call attention to another incident
when Peter let down another net at the command of the Lord,
and enclosed a tremendous amount of fishes. Yet in this
instance the net did not break. You will find the record in
John 21. It is after the resurrection and again Peter and the
disciples had spent a fruitless night fishing, after Peter had
given up all hope that Jesus Christ was coming back again.
He had gone back again to the energy of the flesh, and then
once more Jesus appears on shore, and says to Peter:

"Cast the *net* on the right side of the ship" (John 21:6).

When they had cast the net at Jesus' orders, they enclosed
a net full of great fishes (153 large fish) and,

"For all there were so many, yet was *not* the net broken" (John 21:11).

In this case the net did *not* break. Why not in this case a broken net as in Luke 5? The answer is simply because in the first instance it was done in disobedience, for Jesus had said, "Let down the *nets*," and Simon had let down only one. But in this last instance, Jesus had commanded them to let down only *one* net, and it held. Everything done in the flesh must fail. Only that which is done in complete obedience and faith in the Lord Jesus can succeed. And so Peter had to learn the first great lesson of discipleship, absolute, complete obedience to the will of the Master. Failure to do so can only result in loss.

Now Comes Peter

Now to return to our narrative in Luke 5. When Simon saw the tremendous catch of fishes and the broken net, and the boat sinking under the weight of the catch, he suddenly seemed to come to his senses. He realized what a terrible mistake he had made. He felt the awfulness of his willful, fleshly action, and so we read,

"When *Simon Peter* saw it, he fell down at Jesus' knees, saying, Depart from me; for I am a sinful man, O Lord" (Luke 5:8).

What a tremendously illuminating verse this is! The man who had argued with the Lord, disputed His Word, the man who had sarcastically said, "Because you won't believe me, I'll have to prove it to you, and let down just one net," now falls in repentance at Jesus' feet, confesses his awful sinfulness, repents and calls Him Lord. It is interesting in this connection to note that in verse 5, Simon calls Jesus "Master," and says:

"Master, we have toiled all the night, and have taken nothing."

When Peter comes to the place of complete and full obedience and repentance, however, he drops the name, Master, and he calls Him *Lord*. That is the first requisite of discipleship, to recognize the absolute Lordship of Jesus Christ. Then too, do not miss the point that up until the eighth verse, the name, "Simon" is used each time he is referred to, but when Simon comes to the place of acknowledging Him as Lord, the name, Peter, occurs. This is the new nature which is now coming to the forefront, the new man of the spirit who is willing to follow the Lord Jesus Christ.

This is a passage which carries a tremendous lesson for all of us. The man who had argued with the Lord is now ready to follow Him all the way.

The Crisis In Peter's Life

This was a crisis in Simon's life. Notice carefully that it was Simon who went fishing, it was Simon who caught nothing, it was Simon who disputed with the Lord, but when we read of Simon's repentance, confession, and acknowledgment of Him as Lord, it is Peter who is speaking. Now the new nature reveals itself. Before it had been all flesh, all Simon, Simon, Simon. But now coming to the surface and to the fore, is the new nature, Peter.

Only after the new Peter had gained the victory over the old Simon did Jesus reveal the great lesson He had in mind when He performed this miracle. He was not interested merely in the fish, but in something far more important.

> "And Jesus said unto Simon, Fear not; from henceforth thou shalt catch men" (Luke 5:10).

Here then is a brand new commission, a new experience, an additional blessing. Simon Peter the believer, now becomes Peter the disciple. He had come *to* Jesus for salvation. Now he is to follow *after* Him for service, and we read:

"And when they had brought their ships to land, *they forsook all, and followed Him.*" (Luke 5:11).

They Forsook All

We repeat, salvation is free, and costs us nothing, for it cost Him His *all*. But discipleship is quite a different matter. It means full surrender, complete yielding, a forsaking of self to follow Him. It means absolute, unquestioning obedience to His will. This is the greatest need in the Church of our Lord Jesus Christ today. There are all too few "disciples," who are willing to pay the price of service and victory.

There are thousands of believers, who like Simon before this crisis in his life came, just go on day after day, week after week, without power or fruit, while the few devoted, surrendered disciples, do all the work and sacrificing, and of course, get most of the blame when things go wrong. The average Christian is just a "hitch-hiker" on the way to heaven. A few others have to do the driving, the pushing and the pulling, and the toiling and pay for the gas, while the rest just ride along, singing about salvation, testifying about their glorious Lord, but knowing nothing about discipleship.

It is a matter of history that all the mighty servants of the Lord who were greatly used of God, came in the course of their Christian experience to just such a crisis as Simon did. Subsequent to their conversion they came to the place where the flesh had to be repudiated, to the place where in full and complete surrender they gave their all to Him. And so we ask, is Jesus your Saviour only, or have you also owned Him fully as Lord and Master of your entire life? He wants to be the Lord of your life, because He knows that only in that way can you get the very best He has for you. It is only such whom He will use. It is a matter of record that it is the disciples, those who have owned the Lordship of Christ, who have been used of God in the promotion of the work He has committed to His followers.

May God help us to face the question honestly, for there is a judgment seat of Christ coming, when we shall have to give an account to Him. Am I living a life that is less than God's best for me? Am I missing something the Lord wants me to have? Do I go week after week, month after month, without seeming progress? Is my life without power, fruit, joy and assurance? Then I need the experience of Simon Peter.

Search your own heart, and ask yourself whether there is any progress in your Christian life since you were saved? Do you pray more effectively? Is the Word of God more precious to you? Do you have a greater passion for souls? Is your love for Him warmer now than ever before? Do you witness like you did when you were in your first love? Or has it just been a drab experience, going on day after day, enjoying salvation, but not really working at it? The Bible says, "Work out your own salvation with fear and trembling." Ah, my friend, if your testimony is, that there has been no power in your life, and you need another experience, then let Simon help you.

In these days when we hear so much about revival, and so many unscriptural methods are being used to promote revival, we need to be reminded that revival can only come when the children of God come to the place where they realize what they owe their Lord.

Chapter Six

SALVATION AND DISCIPLESHIP

And he brought him to Jesus.

John 1:42

THIS is Simon's first meeting with the Lord and it resulted in his salvation. When he came *to* the Lord Jesus he was Simon. When he left Jesus, he was Peter. From then on he was Simon Peter. Yes, Andrew brought his brother, Simon, and he became Peter instead.

He was saved but that was all. From the record it seems clear that Simon had gone back to his old job as fisherman, without apparent change of any kind. Then comes Simon Peter's second meeting with his Lord, and what a momentous occasion it became in his life. It was the crisis, the turning point in his career. The record is found in Mark 1:14-18. This meeting in Mark 1 was subsequent to his first meeting in John, when Andrew first brought him to Jesus. When Simon first met Jesus, John the Baptist was still preaching and baptizing at the river Jordan, and it was because John had pointed out Jesus with the words:

"Behold, the Lamb of God, which taketh away the sin of the world" (John 1:29).

that Andrew had followed Jesus, and then went and brought his brother, Simon.

Second Meeting

But this second meeting between Peter and the Lord Jesus recorded in Mark 1, was *after* John had been put in prison.

After Peter's coming *to* Christ for salvation, a time elapses during which John is cast in prison by King Herod for preaching on the matter of divorce. It was not until after this that Peter again meets the Lord Jesus. How much time elapsed between his first and second meetings, we do not know; neither is it important. Here is the record:

"Now *after* that John was put in prison, Jesus came into Galilee, preaching the gospel of the kingdom of God. . .

Now as he walked by the sea of Galilee, he saw Simon and Andrew his brother casting a net into the sea; for they were fishers.

And Jesus said unto them, Come ye *after* me, and I will make you to become fishers of men.

And straightway they forsook their nets, and followed him" (Mark 1:14, 16-18).

We are emphasizing the fact that these two calls of Simon Peter, the first in John which resulted in Simon's coming *to* Christ, and this second call in Mark resulting in Peter's coming *after* Christ, were not the same call. Many do not distinguish between the first call of Peter to come *to* Jesus, and the second call to come *after* Him. Not only were these two calls separated by a period of time, but they differed basicly in their content and result in Peter's life. When Simon came *to* Christ, he *received* something. He received eternal life, he received a new name, a new position, a new nature. But then he went right on living as he had before. He was saved, yes, indeed, but salvation means more than merely being saved from sin and from the judgment of hell.

Coming After Jesus

In this second call, Peter, who had already received something from the Lord Jesus, now leaves all *for* the Lord Jesus and having first come *to* Him for salvation, he now comes *after*

Him for service, and suffering. Coming to Christ results in
salvation; coming *after* Him results in discipleship. Believing
on the Lord Jesus and receiving Him as Saviour does not
make one a disciple; it merely makes one a saint. Until the
believer understands the difference between being a saint
and being a disciple, coming to Christ as Saviour, and following Him as Lord and Master, surrendering all to Him, he
will never know the joy of "the life abundant."

Two Possibilities

One cannot read the Bible very far before coming face to
face with the teaching of these two distinct possibilities of the
Christian life. All through the Bible we find these two kinds
of Christians. Jesus said in John 10:10

> "I am come that they might have life, and that they
> might have it more abundantly."

There is a world of difference between having "life" and
having life "more abundant." You can have life, eternal life,
by simply coming to Jesus Christ, and trusting Him for salvation, but you will never know the "life abundant" until you
have learned to come *after* Him in full surrender and followed
Him as a disciple. To be saved, you receive God's free gift
of grace; to be a disciple you have to return to Him that
which you are. Jesus said:

> "Come unto me, all ye that labour and are heavy laden,
> and I will give you rest" (Matthew 11:28).

That is the "rest" of salvation. It is the gift of God. It is
free. You can do nothing to earn it or obtain it, for it is given
by grace. But Jesus did not stop with this verse, but added
verse 29.

> "*Take* my yoke upon you, and *learn* of me; for I am
> meek and lowly in heart: and ye shall find rest unto
> your souls" (Matthew 11:29).

This is quite another experience, even though the verses occur together. First we are invited to come, to come, to *come*, and I will *give* you rest. This is salvation—the rest of salvation, for which nothing can be paid. It is received as a free gift.

In the very next verse, in Matthew 11:29, however, those who have already come and received the *rest* of salvation, are now invited to bring something. They are invited to "take my yoke, and learn of me." This means a sacrifice—this means paying the price, and results in the abundant life, and the life of victory and of service. This is distinguished in the Bible as discipleship. The word, "discipolos" means "a follower, a student, a learner," one who goes at the command of his teacher.

Two Planes of Christian Experience

There are then two kinds of believers, those who have come to Christ for salvation, and those who have learned the secret of the victorious life by a complete and full yielding and surrender. The first results in salvation, the second results in service. All through the Scriptures we meet up with this tremendous truth, so little understood by the average believer, who goes on day after day, year after year, saved but powerless, weak, wavering, defeated, fruitless, to be saved at last "so as by fire," yet lose the reward at the end of the road. We are not to confuse salvation with discipleship, and so we repeat it over and over again. Salvation is free. We want to be clear on that, because it cost the Lord Jesus His all. But to be a disciple you must be willing to pay the price of "taking his yoke," following in His footsteps, presenting your bodies a living sacrifice, and even if need be, seal your testimony with your blood.

The reason the Church of Christ is so powerless is largely because it is filled with people who are satisfied with

mere salvation from hell, so that they can go to heaven when
they die, but have never caught the vision of service, of complete surrender, and the fulness of the blessing of discipleship.
In addition to mere salvation we should learn the lesson of
discipleship, and the striving for that reward and crown
which we may lay at Jesus' feet.

VICTORY OR DEFEAT

Paul knew the difference between these two kinds of
Christians, and classifies them as *carnal* and *spiritual*. You can
have peace *with* God by just receiving Christ, but you will
never know the peace *of* God until you have learned to turn
everything over to Him who saved you, or as Paul says:

"Be careful for nothing; but in every thing by prayer
and supplication with thanksgiving let your requests be
made known unto God.

And the peace of God, which passeth all understanding
shall keep your hearts and minds through Christ Jesus"
(Philippians 4:6-7).

It is possible, like Israel, to be out of Egypt forever by the
shed blood of the Lamb, but never to reach the Canaan of
the abundant life, and like Israel, to wander in the wilderness
of defeat for forty years. There is a victorious life, and there
is a defeated life. Peace *with* God, and the peace *of* God;
salvation and discipleship; coming *to* Christ and coming *after*
Christ; taking free salvation, and taking the yoke of service;
a coming *to* Christ and a going *for* Christ. We can be in the
light, and yet need to learn to *walk* in the light. How wonderfully Jesus illustrates this truth. In John 4 our Saviour says
to a woman at the well:

"Whosoever drinketh of this water shall thirst again:
But whosoever drinketh of the water that I shall give
him shall never thirst; but the water that I shall give

him shall be in him a well of water springing up into everlasting life" (John 4:13-14).

This is the water of salvation. Every believer has in him the water of life. But if it remains only in him, it goes no further, and it can, of course, benefit no one else. And so there is a progression in John 7 where Jesus says this:

"In the last day, that great day of the feast, Jesus stood and cried, saying, If any man thirst, let him come unto me, and drink" (John 7:37).

This is again referring to salvation, coming to Him for redemption, but our Saviour did not stop there. He added:

"He that believeth on me, as the scripture hath said, *out of his belly shall flow* rivers of living water.

(But this spake he of the Spirit, which they that believe on him should receive: for the Holy Ghost was not yet given; because that Jesus was not yet glorified)" (John 7: 38-39).

Notice the two possibilities clearly set forth here, and kept distinct by our Lord. In John 4 our Saviour promises the woman at the well the living water *within* her, but in John 7 Jesus says, that out of his inward parts *shall flow* rivers of living water. Not rills, not brooks, but *rivers!* This is the abundant life. To have the water *in* you is salvation. Only as you become a disciple, can it flow out, and benefit others.

Simon Peter

We return now to Simon Peter for a closing illustration. In John 1, Simon comes *to* Christ, and was saved, but nothing else seems to have happened as far as the record goes. There was no outward change in his life whatsoever. He went back to his fishing and his nets and his occupation just as before. And then came the second call in Mark 1: "Come ye *after* me," and then we read:

"And straightway they forsook their nets, and followed him" (Mark 1:18).

Simon who had become Peter by coming to Christ now becomes a disciple by heeding His command, and leaving all to follow Him. The same happened to James and to John, for we read in the same chapter:

"And when he had gone a little farther thence, he saw James the son of Zebedee, and John his brother, who also were in the ship mending their nets.

And straightway he called them: and they left their father Zebedee in the ship with the hired servants, and went after him" (Mark 1:19-20).

They left something when *this* call for service came. They left their father, their ships, and the servants, and came after Him. Again we state, and we shall continue to repeat it—salvation is free, for we do not want to be misunderstood on that matter, but discipleship is only for those who are willing to pay the price. We shall study in the next chapter the abundant teaching of the Scriptures concerning the price of discipleship and following the Lord Jesus Christ, and also the glorious reward which awaits at the end of the road.

Now before closing this chapter, may I ask, have you ever heeded Christ's call to come *after* Him? You are saved, you have trusted Him, but you are not fully happy. You are not satisfied, you do not have the assurance and the joy of salvation. Is your life really counting for Christ? Have you ever made a full surrender to Him? Do you know the blessing of a fully yielded life?

I do not care by what name you call it, but there are these two possibilities of Christian experience. We may call it a definite experience, a second blessing, or anything else. We may call it full surrender, or the victorious life, or dedication. We simply will not quibble about the terms, but it is the greatest need of the day. It may or may not be accompanied by emotional thrills; it comes when the believer faces the fact that he owes his all to Him who gave His all for us.

This experience may come simultaneously with and at the same moment we are saved, as happened in the case of Paul. It may come some time later as in the case of Peter. It may be a definite experience when in some crisis we make the full surrender, and make a covenant with God. Or it may be a gradual growth in grace and knowledge, so that we arrive at the place of discipleship almost without being able to remember just when and how it began and how it started and happened. All these details are unimportant. The important thing, the all-important thing, is to ask oneself the honest question, Am I my best for the Lord Jesus Christ? Do I know the joy of discipleship and surrender? Have I yielded everything at His feet? Does my life really count? Then honestly search your heart for all known and doubtful sin, every unyielded, unsurrendered idol. Confess it, dedicate your all, no matter what the price, and the blessing will be yours. Call it by any name you may choose. THIS IS THE ABUNDANT LIFE!

Chapter Seven

THE WAY OF THE CROSS

*Go ye therefore, and teach all nations, baptizing them
in the name of the Father, and of the Son, and of the
Holy Ghost:*
*Teaching them to observe all things whatsoever I have
commanded you*

Matthew 28:19-20.

Our Lord Jesus before He left, gave two commissions to
His disciples. The one was to *preach* the Gospel. The other
was to *teach* those who had already received the Gospel, and
had been saved. The first commission is familiar to all of you:

"Go ye into all the world, and preach the gospel to
every creature" (Mark 16:15).

This Gospel is the message of the good news that Jesus
died for our sins, and arose from the dead for our justification,
that all who believe in Him receive eternal life. But there
is more to it than just being saved; there is more to it than
just escaping hell; there is more to it than going to heaven
when we die. Salvation is only the beginning of something
which will consummate when Jesus comes. And so our
Lord gave an additional commission when He said:

"Go ye therefore, and *teach* all nations. . ." (Matthew
28:19).

This is an additional commission to the *preaching* of the
Gospel. The word, "teach," in Matthew 28:19 is *"matheteuo,"*
and means "to make disciples." A disciple is a pupil, an

57

apprentice, a learner, in preparation for a specific task. We are not only saved *from* something, but *for* and *unto* something as well. Discipleship involves sacrifice, it means discipline. Peter, we have already seen, had to learn this important lesson before he could be used to the full by his Saviour. When he came *to* Christ in John 1, he became a believer. When he left all and came *after* Christ, He became a disciple.

Two Ministries

There are, then, two ministries which God has committed to those whom He has entrusted with the Gospel. The one is to go out and tell the good news of salvation, and the other is to follow up this preaching of the Gospel with an indoctrination and a teaching of those who have already believed. The purpose of God in saving men is not only to keep them from going to hell, and taking them to heaven when they die, but to use them for service in reaching others while here below. It is a fact, taught definitely in the Scriptures, and corroborated by all the experiences of the Christian church throughout the ages, that the only people God really uses in the carrying out of His commission, and in the fulfilling of His program, are those who in addition to having come to Christ as Saviour, have also learned the great lesson of His Lordship, and have owned Him as the absolute Master of their whole lives, and have come to the place of complete and full and definite surrender of all they are and have for His service. This is called discipleship.

Paying the Price

Before going on to the price of true discipleship, we want to be perfectly clear on the matter of salvation. We fear that when we preach discipleship, folks often confuse it with salvation, and get the idea they must do something, leave something, give up something, to be saved. This is the result of preaching a gospel which does not distinguish thoroughly between salvation and discipleship.

Again and again we have folks using those passages where Christ speaks of following Him, as though it were the condition for their own salvation. And, this of course, is appealing to the natural heart and the flesh. Man likes to have a finger in the pie of his salvation, and anyone who promises him a little part, be it ever so small, either in obtaining his salvation or in retaining it, is sure to find a great many eager ears who would like to have just a little part of the glory of their own redemption.

We must, therefore, keep on emphasizing, that salvation is all the work of God. It is of the Lord, and we can do nothing, or add anything to it. When you come to Christ you bring nothing, because you have nothing, but instead you receive everything. It is all of grace through faith. But to be a disciple is quite another matter. It means to follow in the steps of the Master. It involves a complete surrender to His will, an acknowledgment of His Lordship.

It costs something to be a disciple, while to be a believer is free. The word, "disciple," means "a follower, a learner or a student," one who obeys orders. When you follow Him, you become an apprentice of the Man of Sorrows, and His steps will lead through Gethsemane and up to the Hill of Calvary. To be a disciple means that you must be willing to pay the price that Christ Himself paid.

Right here is where so much gospel preaching fails. It confuses salvation with discipleship, faith with works, coming to Christ to be saved, and coming after Him to serve. We have heard a great many sermons which left the impression that to be saved one must give up this thing, and give up that thing, and do this and do that, pay the price and forsake all. But that is not salvation. You are not saved because you have done a thing or left a thing, or felt anything. You are saved because Jesus paid the price for your sin on Calvary. You are saved because He left His all, to give you eternal life.

You are not saved by what you feel, but by what He felt on the Cross of Calvary for you. But you may have all that and still die in the wilderness, out of Egypt and short of God's best in Canaän for you. You may have salvation, which comes by believing, and yet come short of God's very best for you.

THE MEANING OF ETERNAL LIFE

The life of discipleship and following the Lord involves not only a full surrender and a yielding, but it involves suffering, and it may even mean paying the price of life itself. Then, too, eternal life is given as the permanent possession, and is independent of anything you do or will do. To have eternal life will bring you to heaven at last.

It is a different proposition with the life of the disciple, and the abundant life, however. While it assures one of a reward for faithfulness in His Kingdom when the Lord comes again, there is always the warning that it is possible to lose one's *discipleship,* if we fail to realize that only by complete and full and perfect obedience to Him can it be retained. John tells us in an interesting verse in II John 8:

> "Look to yourselves, that we lose not those things which we have *wrought,* but that we receive a full reward."

Notice in this verse that he does not say, "Look to yourselves that we lose not those things which we have *received,*" but "those things which *we have wrought.*" John is not speaking of losing the gift of God, salvation, but the reward which the Lord will give for faithful service. Some will merely be saved. Others will receive a full reward. He is speaking about the things *we* have wrought, the things *we* have done for Christ. Discipleship then means sacrifice and suffering, but also promises reward and joy. There are many, many passages in Scripture which deal with the distinction between merely believing and being a disciple. We call your attention to only a few. In Matthew 8:19 we read:

"And a certain scribe came, and said unto him, Master, I will follow thee whithersoever thou goest."

Here was a man who evidently had already come *to* Christ, and now offers to come *after* Him, to follow Him. Notice the answer of our Lord. It is in essence this: "Have you counted the cost? Do you know what it involves to follow Me and become a disciple? Do you realize what you are promising?" Hear the startling words, therefore, of our Saviour:

"And Jesus saith unto him, The foxes have holes, and the birds of the air have nests; but the Son of Man hath not where to lay his head" (Matthew 8:20).

I imagine the Lord must then have turned to this man and said, "Now do you still want to follow me? Are you willing to pay that price? You must, if you follow Me, follow a rejected Saviour who is on the way to the Cross."

"And another of his disciples said unto him, Lord suffer me first to go and bury my father.

But Jesus said unto him, Follow me; and let the dead bury their dead" (Matthew 8:21-22).

"If you want to be My disciple," says Jesus, "you must be willing to subject *everything* to me, placing Me before everything else, no matter how important other things may seem, even the burial of your own father." Now, of course, Jesus did not mean that we are not to give due respect to our loved ones, and there certainly is no harm in burying one's father, but He tested him to see if he was willing to go *all* the way with Him. The business of a disciple is not burying dead people, but raising the dead by the Gospel of the grace of God. In Mark 8:34 the Lord Jesus Christ says:

"Whosoever will come after me, let him deny himself, and take up his cross, and follow me."

In Luke 14:27 we read

"And whosoever doth not bear his cross, and come after me, cannot be my disciple."

Our Lord does not say you *must* bear the cross to be *saved*, but to be *a disciple*. There is only one Cross in Scripture. We speak of *crosses* in the plural, but Scripture recognizes only one, and that is the Cross on which Jesus Himself died. It is the cross of service for others. And if you want to be a disciple you will have to bear that cross, for you must seek first the glory of God and be more concerned with the salvation of your fellowmen than merely enjoying your own salvation in Christ.

We all talk about crosses. A man said to me one day, "I have a terrible cross to bear. I married a woman who has a disposition that would make a tigress look tame. I have a terrible cross."

I said, "Brother, that is not your cross; that was your own mistake."

Another said, "I have a cross to bear. One of my children is an invalid, and it ties me down so that I cannot do what I would like to do for Christ."

Again, that is not a cross. That is a burden which the Lord has laid upon you, and one He offers to share with you.

Still another says, "I have a great cross to bear. Before I was saved I had a terrible appetite for liquor and now the Lord has put me in a business where I have to meet men all day long who tempt me to go back to the old life. Yes, it is a heavy cross."

Listen, brother, that, too, is not a cross. That is a trial and a test of your faith. The Lord Himself will give you the victory. The Cross in Scripture is only one, the Cross on which Christ hung. To carry the cross means to die. Are you willing to carry that Cross? That is the price of discipleship. When Christian men and women learn to carry that Cross, there will be a revival that will shake the very foundation of the earth.

DENY THYSELF

Again Jesus said, "If any man will be my disciple, let him deny himself." This is quite a different thing from self-denial. Self-denial is just withholding some things from yourself that possibly you are better off without anyway. But "denying self" is to offer *yourself* to the Lord for His service.

It means rather "putting yourself on the cross as a living sacrifice." That is what Paul says in Romans 12:1

> "I beseech you, therefore, brethren, by the mercies of God, that ye present your bodies a living sacrifice, holy, acceptable unto God, which is your reasonable service."

Literally interpreted it means, "making a present of your bodies to God as a living sacrifice in gratitude to Him who was your dying sacrifice to save you." We hear people say, "I am ready to die for Christ, I love Him so much." But He does not ask us to do that. He does not ask us to die for Him. He wants us to live for Him. I would rather not die for Christ. I would much rather live for Him as long as possible. The trouble is there are some Christians who are willing to die for Christ, but they are not living their life for Him now.

Many other passages might be quoted to show the price of discipleship which the Lord lays down. But before concluding, I would simply remind you that Jesus who makes these demands would never ask anyone to do anything which He Himself was not willing to do. He, too, when He came to save us, made everything else secondary to the business of obeying His Father. He became the true exemplary Disciple and left *all* that He might save us.

Think of who He was, the Creator of the universe! And yet out of His love for poor, lost, good-for-nothing, hell-deserving sinners He was willing to leave heaven's glory, and come to be despised, forsaken, spit upon, and crucified on the Cross that we might live. We certainly should not hesitate for a single moment when He says to us, "Come ye after Me, and I will make you to become fishers of men." Do you want to meet Him without bringing Him the best that you have been able to? God help us to say, "I surrender all."

Remember, if you are a Christian, you are either carnal or spiritual; you are victorious or defeated, and God has something better for you. This is the great need of today, for those who are living a defeated life. If you this very moment will turn everything over to Him, and come in complete and full and absolute surrender with a full confession of all your sins, you will receive that wondrous blessing. You have but to turn to Him now, and do what Peter did — be willing to say "Lord, I will to follow Thee all the way." Then you, too, will experience the abundant life, and become a disciple.

Chapter Eight

THE WAY OF THE BACKSLIDER

And Simon Peter stood and warmed himself. They said therefore unto him, Art not thou also one of his disciples? He denied it, and said, I am not.

John 18:25

IN the preceding chapters we have pointed out in detail the difference between salvation and discipleship. When we come to the Lord Jesus in faith we receive eternal life, but only when we learn to acknowledge Him as *Lord* of all we are and possess, can we know the joy of full surrender and discipleship.

We have also seen that Peter had two calls, one to come *to* Christ for salvation, and another to come *after* the Lord for service and sacrifice. We also pointed out the price of discipleship, which means a complete yielding and owning of Him as the director, the Master, the Lord of our life, willing to obey orders no matter where they may lead, in the absolute confidence that He also is able to "keep that which we have committed unto Him against that day."

DISCIPLESHIP MAY BE LOST

We must of necessity make another distinction between salvation and discipleship. For while salvation gives eternal life, discipleship may be lost. It is possible for a Christian who has known complete victory in Christ to lose that very victory and joy of discipleship, just because, while salvation

65

depends upon faith, discipleship depends upon the *faithfulness* of the believer.

As a striking example of this we take again the life of Peter who lost that abundant life when the real test came. After three years of following Christ, in which he saw all the evidences of His power and majesty, Jesus now with His disciples is nearing the Cross. In a valiant but unwise attempt to defend his Lord in the Garden of Gethsemane, Peter had drawn his sword and cut off the ear of the servant of the High Priest. But in spite of his efforts to defend his Master, they had taken the Lord in the Garden and having bound Him led Him away, and it was then that Peter's courage failed completely, and the next thing we read is this:

"Peter followed *afar off*."

Peter was still following, but he had dropped behind, for we are told that he followed *afar off*. Finally they come to the High Priest's palace, and Peter, cold and numb from following afar off, is singled out as one of the followers of the Lord. In John 18:17 we read:

"Then saith the damsel that kept the door unto Peter, Art not thou also one of this man's disciples? He saith, I am not."

Notice the question, "Art not thou one of this man's *disciples?*" Again in John 18:25 we have the second instance of Peter's denial of Christ.

"And Simon Peter stood and warmed himself. They said therefore unto him, Art not thou also one of His disciples? He denied it, and said, I am not."

Matthew adds the details, how Peter cursed and swore as he denied his Saviour and said, "I don't even know Him."

"Then began he to curse and to swear, saying I know not the man" (Matt. 26:74).

A DISCIPLE NO LONGER

What a sad, sad picture! Peter, a follower of the Lord, once more giving way to the old man of the flesh, Simon, cursing and swearing that he did not even know the Man who was to die for him. Right then and there Peter lost his discipleship. He did not lose his salvation; he lost his discipleship. He lost his joy and his fellowship with the Lord. He was not cast out, nor did he cease to be a child of God, but he lost the victory of discipleship.

The next thing we see is Peter crushed by the consciousness of his loss slipping outside and weeping bitterly. But for all the weeping Peter did on that night it availed him nought. It brought him no relief and Peter was still as miserable as he was before, even after he had wept bitterly. We often suppose that when Peter went outside and wept that it fixed everything up all right, but it did nothing of the kind. Peter had publicly denied his Lord, and until public sins are publicly confessed, there can be no return of joy and fellowship. We do not mean by this that we must confess our private sins to one another, but a public reproach calls for a public confession.

Maybe Peter also had the notion, which so many have, that we can backslide and deny our Lord, and then if we just confess it in private and in secret, everything is going to be taken care of. No, there is a principle involved here which goes very deep. It is this, and we repeat it again—public sins must be publicly confessed. Let me emphasize, however, that this does not include private sins. Private sins, we believe, must be privately confessed, but the other is equally as true—public sins should be publicly confessed.

Many a church has died of dry rot just because they have not insisted upon public confession and discipline of those who have been a public reproach to the cause of Christ. Too often, when Christians have backslidden and brought disgrace upon the church, they are quietly welcomed back again, and because they have influence or money, the thing is smoothed over and passed by. But our precious Lord would do no such thing with Peter, for he believes in doing everything in a thorough way. And so, weep as much as Peter would, this thing had been committed in the open, and must be confessed in the open.

And Peter

Peter lost his discipleship publicly and his repentance in a corner could not help him. But he was still a believer, and the object of the love of Christ. He was still a child of God, though in sad condition, and though he had denied his Lord, his Lord did not cast him away, but went about to bring him back.

I want you to notice how tenderly the Lord went about this entire business. After His death our Saviour arose and appeared unto the women. And to these women the angels at the tomb had a message for the disciples, and we hear them saying:

"Be not affrighted! Ye seek Jesus of Nazareth, which was crucified: He is risen; He is not here: behold the place where they laid him.

But go your way, tell His disciples *and Peter* that he goeth before you into Galilee. . ." (Mark 16:6-7).

Tell His disciples *and Peter*. Notice the message the angels gave the women. The disciples, *and Peter*. We notice from this that Peter is not classed with the disciples any more, even though he had wept bitterly and tried to repent in secret for his public sin. How it must have cut Peter to the heart as the women bore the message, "We were commanded to bring the news to the disciples *and to you, Peter.*" He had lost his discipleship, his victory, his joy, but he had not lost his Saviour. Thank God for that! Tenderly, yet emphatically and cuttingly, the Lord reminds him with these two words, "and Peter," that while he was no longer a disciple, yet the Lord was thinking of him and only waiting for him to meet the conditions of confession and repentance to be restored. In these words, therefore, there is both rebuke and an invitation.

I Go Fishing

Several days passed, during which the Lord had showed Himself to the disciples *and Peter,* but Peter was still miserable as every backslider is, no matter how cleverly it may be covered up. And so we read how Peter in desperation and misery, decides there is no use going on any more, and he might just as well try and forget the Lord entirely, forget the past, and return to his old life, and his old occupation. John gives us the graphic description of this attempt on the part of Peter in chapter 21:

> "There were together Simon Peter, and Thomas called Didymus, and Nathanael of Cana in Galilee, and the sons of Zebedee, and two other of his disciples.
>
> Simon Peter saith unto them, I go a fishing. They say unto him, We also go with thee. They went forth, and entered into a ship immediately; and that night they caught nothing" (John 21:2-3).

Simon Peter saith, "I go a fishing." I can almost imagine Peter saying, "It's all over, men. There's no use going on anymore. The Lord is risen, we know that; but where is He now? We see Him once in a while, but He isn't preaching anymore. He doesn't seem to have any more mission down here below. He isn't mingling with the crowds as he did of yore. Surely the Kingdom hope is all gone, and we might just as well forget about the whole business, and go back to our old jobs again."

Peter had left all on the occasion of his becoming a disciple and had promised to follow the Lord all the way. He and the others had left their old life, and even their old occupation over three and one-half years before, when they had heard Him say, "Come ye after Me, and I will make you to become fishers of men."

Poor, poor Simon Peter! How blind sin does make even the believer. All he needed to do to be restored and have everything all right was to seek the Lord and make his public confession, and all would be made right again. But the backslider does not seek after the Lord. The moment he does he is not backslidden any more. Thank God, however, that the Lord does seek the backslider! So here we find Peter going fishing, without the Lord. The sad thing is that Simon Peter induced six other disciples to go with him.

Christians never backslide alone. They crave company, and always drag others along. That is characteristic of those who get out of fellowship. If Peter had only gone alone it would have been better for him and for all. It is a fact which we have experienced over and over again in our ministry, and to which every preacher, I am sure, will testify, that when Christians become sour and bitter and backslidden, instead of keeping it to themselves, they always try to get everyone else to backslide with them. Instead of leaving the church where they can no longer get a blessing and permitting the ones who still are in fellowship to get the blessing, they hang around the back of the church whispering and criticizing and finding fault until they have a whole group upset over trivialities of their own.

THEY CAUGHT NOTHING

And that night they caught nothing, *nothing*. They fished all night but to no avail. Without Jesus there is no use fishing. Yet, Christians insist on fishing when out of fellowship with their Lord. They still shout and pray and preach, but nothing happens. This is characteristic. But, "that night they caught nothing." After Jesus met them the next morning, they caught more fish than they could drag to the shore.

Have I described your condition, and are you willing to be honest enough to face up to it? You too were on fire for the Lord once, and had zeal and joy in His service, and now you too have become bitter, and critical, and sour, and fault-finding.

I have heard all the excuses. Someone else has injured you, someone else has failed. But beloved, when we face the thing thoroughly before the Lord, as Peter had to face it, we will have to confess that we are to blame. And if we are willing to be obedient to Him, then no matter what anyone else in all the world may do, we can still be in fellowship with Him. May God grant us to take these lessons of Peter to our own heart, and to claim the promise:

"If we confess our sins, He is faithful and just to forgive us our sins, and to cleanse us from all unrighteousness" (I John 1:9).

Chapter Nine

IF WE CONFESS OUR SINS

But if we walk in the light, as he is in the light, we have fellowship one with another, and the blood of Jesus Christ his Son cleanseth us from all sin

I John 1:7.

IN the foregoing chapters we have studied the discipleship of the Apostle, Simon Peter. After walking in sweet fellowship with the Lord for three and one-half years as a disciple, Peter failed when the real test came. He denied his Lord and lost his discipleship and fell from fellowship. But the remarkable thing is, that the Lord Jesus Christ still loved him and remembered him. It was He who gave him that look in the midst of his deep agony which caused Peter to go outside and to weep bitterly.

We do thank God that in spite of Peter's denial of the Lord, the Lord did not deny him. He was still a child of God, even though he had lost his joy and the victory and fellowship. So far did Peter go, that he finally proposed to go back to his old life of fishing, and persuaded six of his fellows to go with him. But although they fished all that night, they caught nothing, and the morning found them without even so much as enough fish for a meal. Hungry and tired, but not yet convinced of the fact that fishing without Christ is always fruitless, they were pulling for the shore when something suddenly happened.

72

"But when the morning was now come, Jesus stood on the shore: but the disciples knew not that it was Jesus.

Then Jesus saith unto them, Children, have ye any meat? They answered him, No" (John 21:4-5).

There is both irony and gracious tenderness in this simple record. Of course, the Lord knew that they had caught nothing, but to make them understand that without Him nothing can avail, He asked the question in this ironic way, "Children, have ye any meat?"

How it must have cut them to their very heart. These men, who had tried to forget about the Lord, are now suddenly confronted by Him, and this word of rebuke is the first that falls from His lips.

There is another lesson here, however, a lesson of graciousness and tenderness toward His erring disciples. While He had been unseen to them, He had seen them, toiling and sweating all night in their fruitless, fleshly efforts. Then He comes to meet them on the shore in the morning. No wonder the disciples did not recognize Him at first. A believer out of fellowship has his whole reason and judgment twisted and warped. With what a sting of a guilty conscience the words must have fallen on them, "Children, have ye any meat?"

Notice He calls them, not men, but "children." They had acted like children, little babies, and not as mature believers, who had walked with the Saviour and followed Him for three and one-half years. There is a tenderness here, but also stinging rebuke. "Children, have ye any meat?" "Have ye any meat?" Of course, the Lord knew all about this. It was not to get information for Himself, but to produce conviction in their own hearts. Then follows the command of the Lord:

"Cast the net on the right side of the ship, and ye shall

find. They cast therefore, and now they were not able to draw it for the multitude of fishes" (John 21:6).

"Cast the net on the right side of the ship." When you are out of fellowship with the Lord, you are always fishing on the wrong side, no matter which side that may happen to be, and he says "try the right side." Now in obedience to the Lord they inclosed a multitude of fishes. When that happened John recognized the Lord, and exclaimed, "It is the Lord." It was John who recognized Him but poor Peter was caught utterly unawares. In his efforts to fix up the old skiff for his fishing trip, he had sacrificed everything he had, even all that he wore. Peter was naked and without clothes. He had evidently used his clothing to calk the seams of the old boat and his shirt to plug the holes, for when the Lord surprised them that morning, we read in the record, "Peter was naked."

Once he had said, I will leave everything for Thee, and then he had failed to stand the test. Now he had given everything to go back to his old life, until he did not even have a stitch of clothes on his back. It may be, too, that Peter had been working hard, and in the heat of the toil he had removed all of his clothing. Yes, sometimes men will work harder in the flesh than they do in the spirit. I have known those who were zealous for the Lord and the church, and then when something happened which broke that fellowship, they have been twice as active and did twice as much to break down that very program they were once so zealous in serving.

Your Eyes on Jesus

Strange what happens when men get their eyes off the Lord and fix them on others, and go forward in the energy of the flesh. Strange what happens when we follow Jesus afar off and get our eyes on troubles and the faults of others, and our problems, instead of on Christ. And so we read the intriguing record:

"Now when Simon Peter heard that it was the Lord, he girt his fisher's coat unto him, (for he was naked,) and did cast himself into the sea" (John 21:7).

Then follows that memorable scene about the beach fire, and that never-to-be-forgotten breakfast with the Lord Jesus as the host. Jesus had prepared food for these hungry disciples and invited them to come and dine. Jesus, knowing that they had caught nothing all night, had already anticipated the need of these hungry fishermen, and had fish frying on the coals when they stepped out of the boat. From the record it seems that the meal was eaten in absolute silence. Not a word seems to have been spoken. There is no record that any of them had a word to say. What could they possibly say? Here they were, face to face with the Lord whom they had forsaken, and with Peter who had cursed and sworn that he knew not the Lord.

It was best that nothing be said. The less said, the better. Just let the experience sink home. So the Lord Himself also said nothing while they were eating. What a strange breakfast it must have been! Here were these disciples with their Lord, and not one word spoken between them. But then, when the meal was ended, the Lord Jesus turns to Simon Peter. He singles him out—he who had denied Him, and was the instigator of this outlaw fishing trip, and we read,

"So when they had dined, Jesus saith to Simon Peter, Simon, son of Jonas, lovest thou me more than these?" (John 21:15).

In the light of what we have been teaching concerning the two natures in Simon Peter, this verse is one of the most illuminating which we can possibly find. How meaningful

the way in which the Lord addresses Peter! He calls him
Simon. He does not say unto him, Peter. He does not say
unto him, Simon Peter, but He says, Simon, and then adds
significantly, son of Jonas. Simon was his natural name, by
his first birth. Peter was his spiritual name by his second birth.
Simon was the name he had received from his father, Peter
was the name he had been given by the Lord Himself. One
was the name of the old man, and the other was the name
of the new man. It was when, in the sixteenth chapter of
Matthew, Simon had confessed that Jesus was the Christ, the
Son of God, that Jesus had given him the new name, and had
said:

> "Blessed art thou, Simon Bar-jona: for flesh and blood
> hath not revealed it unto thee, but my Father which is
> in heaven.

> And I say unto thee, That thou art *Peter*, and upon this
> Rock I will build my church" (Matthew 16:17-18).

Simon, son of John! How the Lord reminds him that he
is still *Simon,* that he has given way to the flesh and the old
nature. But is it not wonderful to know also that in spite
of all this, he was still *Peter*. Though Peter seemed to be
completely submerged, he was still there. How wonderful, and
how faithful He is! "If we are unfaithful, He abideth faithful.
He cannot deny Himself."

Peter's Restoration

After the Lord had reminded him of this fact, He says to
him,

> "Simon, son of Jonas, lovest thou me more than these?"

We ask the question, "More than what?" What did our
Lord mean by these words? We believe the answer is quite
evident.

"Do you love Me more than your old life; more than these

old boats and nets; more than these companions and friends?
Three years ago, Peter, you said you would follow Me whereever I went, you gave up everything, but you couldn't go
beyond Gethsemane with Me. You have failed, and gone back
to the love of the old life. Listen, Simon, I want you to come
back to Me. Do you love Me more than these things you have
gone back to? Do you love Me more than anything else?
More than your life, your safety, your comfort?"

Poor Peter, humbled and beaten, was not able to say
this. Bible scholars know that the word, "love," which the
Lord used in this connection to Peter is the word, "agapas,"
meaning "to love above all other things." When Peter gave
answer to the Lord, he did not use "agapas," but a weaker
word for love, "phileo," which means "to be fond of" but is
short of loving above all things, and loving to the limit.

Yes, Peter was coming back. He had lost his boastfulness.
Once he had said, "I will go into death with thee." Now
Jesus asks, "Will you still do it?" and Peter dares not say it
now, but answers, "Yea, Lord, thou knowest that I love you."
But he uses the weaker word, and says, "Not as much as I
ought, but I do love you, Lord."

Then the Lord the second time uses the word, "agapas"
and again Peter cringes and answers with the weaker word,
"phileo." Then the Lord, seeing that Peter is thoroughly
humbled, and ready to confess and come back, stoops to
Peter's word, "phileo," instead of "agapas" in the third time
He speaks to Peter, "Simon, son of John, lovest thou me?"
When the Lord stooped to use Peter's word, and seemed to
say, Do you love me, even a little bit, Peter?, it was too much
for this grieving disciple, and we read in John 21:17

"Peter was grieved because he said unto him the third
time, lovest thou me?"

Three times Peter had publicly denied the Lord. Three times he must publicly confess Him. His weeping outside the door that night had not been enough. Wrongs must be righted. Restitution must be made. True repentance never seeks to hide itself or spare itself, but welcomes the opportunity to make amends and right the wrongs. Repentance must be whole-hearted, sincere, and if need be, willing to pay the price. That is the only kind of repentance that will bring restoration of the abundant life.

Go To Work

Then Jesus tells Peter what he must expect to pay, if he is to follow Him again. When Peter had confessed, our Saviour says:

> "Verily, verily, I say unto thee, When thou wast young, thou girdest thyself, and walkedst whither thou wouldest: but when thou shalt be old, thou shalt stretch forth thy hands, and another shall gird thee, and carry thee whither thou wouldest not.
>
> This spake he, signifying by what death he should glorify God" (John 21:18-19).

Peter, here is the price that you will have to pay if you want to come back! And tradition tells us that Peter himself died by crucifixion some years later. And after the Lord had laid down the terms to Peter, He said,

Follow Me

Follow Me! That was our Lord's final command. Follow Me again, Peter. As far as the Bible record goes, Peter never went fishing again. But we see him a month later at Pentecost with the fire of God in his heart, and the flame of love in his eyes, preaching fearlessly this same Jesus whom he had denied, and three thousand were won for Christ.

Peter never forgot that experience and never departed so far from the Lord again.

Now we should make this practical in our own lives. Will you ask yourself the question, as I want to ask myself the question today, How many of us have been like Simon Peter, once knowing the joy of the Lord and happy in the service, and then something happened? You, of course, feel that you have been wronged, I know, and that it was not your fault. The fact of the matter is, however, that you are not happy, and if *your* life was right, then the wrongs of others would not affect your service and fellowship with Christ. Why not face up to the facts right now? The old Simon has had the upper hand, and Peter has gone down. Defending yourself in your hapless condition, justifying yourself will not settle the matter. Only as we heed the words of Scripture:

"If we confess our sin"

can we find a restoration of our former joy and peace.

Then remember, too, you will not have to answer for someone else's faults. "Unto his own Master every man standeth or falleth." Let us, therefore, be honest with the Lord. Do you pray as much as you used to? Do you? Do you study your Bible as you used to when you were in your first love? Are you too busy, probably even with religious duties? How long since you have won a soul for Christ?

Have you lost that abundant life, that victory, that discipleship which comes by following our Lord, and not men? Following Jesus means Gethsemane and Calvary. Oh, today the Lord is looking for men and women who will follow Him all the way. This is the greatest need of the church today, men and women fully yielded to Him, accepting the abundant life, and bringing on the revival which God knows we need so desperately in these days.

Chapter Ten

THE NEW MESSAGE OF JESUS

When Jesus came into the coasts of Caesarea Philippi, he asked his disciples, saying, Whom do men say that I the Son of man am?

Matthew 16:13

THE time had come in our Lord's ministry to reveal to His disciples a brand new truth about which they as yet knew absolutely nothing. It was the revelation concerning the Church, the Body of Christ, which He would call out after His death and resurrection on the day of Pentecost. In this chapter (Matthew 16) we have the first mention of the word, "church," in the entire Scriptures. To prepare the hearts of the disciples for this brand new revelation He asks the question of His disciples, "Whom do men say that I the Son of man am?"

This question was not prompted by a desire to know what people thought about Him, for He knew all that from the beginning. But it was asked to get from Peter the confession which would provide the setting for this new revelation concerning the Church.

PETER'S ANSWER

After the disciples had told Jesus the various opinions of men concerning Him, He asks the second question:

"But whom say ye that I am?" (Matthew 16:15)

80

To this question it is again Simon Peter who answers without hesitation or doubt:

"Thou art the Christ, the Son of the living God" (Matthew 16:16).

This was the answer the Lord was trying to evoke from him, and having received it, He now makes the new revelation that He is *not* going to set up His earthly kingdom at this time at all, but rather, the nation of Israel and the Kingdom are to be set aside, and He will build His Church. Then follows the amazing answer which stunned the disciples momentarily, and left them in confusion and despair. After Peter's confession, Jesus says to him:

"Blessed art thou, Simon Bar-jona: for flesh and blood hath not revealed it unto thee, but my Father which is in heaven.

And I say also unto thee, That thou art Peter, and upon this rock I will build my church; and the gates of hell (hades) shall not prevail against it" (Matthew 16: 17-18).

Before looking at this first mention of the Church, will you notice how disappointing and confusing this new revelation must have been to His disciples in the light of what they already knew. They as yet knew nothing about the Church. All they had looked forward to and expected was the setting up of the millennial kingdom. When Jesus had called them, they knew He was the Messiah, and they believed He would deliver Israel from the Roman oppression, restore the Kingdom of Israel again, and sit upon the Throne of David in Jerusalem, to reign as King and Messiah according to all the promises given in the Old Testament. They had heard the Kingdom message, "Repent, for the Kingdom of heaven is at hand." Again and again they had asked Him *when* He would declare

Himself, and begin His conquest and reign. Even after His death and resurrection, at His ascension, they still carried this hope, and asked Him their last and final question before He ascended:

"Lord, wilt thou, *at this time* restore again the kingdom to Israel?" (Acts 1:6)

THE MESSIANIC HOPE

This was the Messianic hope held by the disciples and all believing Jews of Jesus' day. They did not expect their Messiah to die on a Cross, but rather to sit on the Throne of David. This is evident from the entire record. But now the time had come to prepare His disciples for the great shock, that the Kingdom was not now to be set up, but instead He would be crucified, and leave them again, and during the interval the Church would be called out as His Bride.

Immediately after the declaration of our Lord Jesus concerning the Church, and His words, "Upon this rock, I will build my church," He continues to tell His followers what lay ahead. What follows is tremendously significant, therefore. Verse 21 of Matthew 16 continues:

"From *that time forth* began Jesus to shew unto his disciples, how that he must go unto Jerusalem, and suffer many things of the elders and chief priests and scribes, *and be killed,* and be raised again the third day."

This was too much for poor Peter, who just a moment before had confessed Him as the Messiah. The Messiah be *killed?* Unthinkable! Impossible! Preposterous! Why, all the prophets had foretold the glorious reign of the Messiah when He would come, and the prophecies are replete with the glowing description of the glory of that day when the King should reign and prosper in Jerusalem. And now Jesus says He must be killed? This was too much for Peter. He seems to say, "What, no kingdom? No reigning with Thee?" Evidently Jesus did not know the Scriptures, and needed some instruction (according to Peter) and so he immediately and promptly offers it:

> "Then Peter took him, and began to rebuke him, saying, Be it far from thee, Lord: this shall not be unto thee" (Matthew 16:22).

Good old Peter! Let us not be too severe on him, for he acted not only on the impulse of the moment, but also on the only light he possessed. He meant every word of what he said, and was sincere in his statement, for Peter understood not yet the mystery of the Church age, the setting aside of the kingdom during this dispensation of grace. Today, nineteen hundred years later, many, many believers are still as confused as Peter concerning the difference between the Kingdom and the Church. They, too, do not see the difference, but refer to the Church as the Kingdom, and imagine that the calling out of the Church cancels the promises and hope of an earthly millennial Kingdom for Israel when Jesus shall come again. How absolutely necessary, therefore, the teaching of our Lord concerning this revelation which confused the disciples, and is still confusing to so many today.

SUGGESTION OF SATAN

What Peter did not know was that the rebuke he made was suggested by the devil himself. Satan would like to have Jesus by-pass the Cross, and go immediately to the Kingdom, just as the disciples expected He would do. And so Jesus answers Peter:

> "But he turned, and said unto Peter, Get thee behind me, Satan: thou art an offence unto me: for thou savourest not the things that be of God, but those that be of men" (Matthew 16:23).

Then Jesus elaborates on the price which His followers will have to pay as a result of His rejection:

"Then said Jesus unto His disciples, If any man will come *after me,* let him deny himself, and take up his cross, and follow me" (Matthew 16:23).

The path to the Kingdom, says Jesus, is by the way of the Cross. Now the full meaning of all this would not be made known until after the day of Pentecost. Here He merely announces the fact. In our passage in Matthew 16 Jesus merely announces the fact of the Church, and that He will be rejected, and that the Church will be built by Him, during the time the Kingdom is postponed. These disciples knew nothing about the message of the Gospel for the Church. They had preached the Kingdom message:

"Repent ye, for the kingdom of heaven is at hand."

It was the offer of the Kingdom to the nation of Israel, on the condition of their acceptance of their Messiah, which they had been told to preach. But we know that in the foreknowledge of God, Israel was to reject this offer, and so we read in John 1:11,

"He came unto his own, and his own received him not."

The nation rejected the King and His message, and as a result the nation was temporarily set aside, the Kingdom postponed, and in the interim the Church, the mystery of other ages, is to be called out.

THE NEW MESSAGE

We cannot, therefore, blame the disciples for not understanding the new revelation concerning the Church. They had preached the Kingdom message to Israel. Surely no one can dispute the fact that the commission Jesus gave to His disciples was not the message for the Church today. It was to Israel, for Israel, and Israel only, and had to do with the offer of the Kingdom and not with Church truth. In Matthew 10 Jesus had given this commission:

> "And when he had called unto him his twelve disciples, he gave them power against unclean spirits, to cast them out, and to heal all manner of sickness and all manner of disease" (Matthew 10:1).

Dare any one claim this is our commission today? Yet it is constantly quoted by those who understand neither the message of the Kingdom nor the message of grace, and claim that these gifts, to cast out demons, heal disease, are for the church today. We have but to read on and we shall see how this violates the simplest rules of Bible interpretation.

After giving the names of the twelve apostles (Matthew 10: 2-4), in order to emphasize that this was an apostolic commission, and these gifts were apostolic, we read in verse 5:

> "These twelve Jesus sent forth, and *commanded them*, saying, *go not* into the way of the Gentiles, and into any city of the Samaritans enter ye not:
>
> But go rather to the lost sheep of the house of Israel" (Matthew 10:5-6).

Could anything be plainer than this? A child is able to understand this. This commission Jesus gave was *not* for the Gentiles nor for the Church, but exclusively for Israel. To quote from this passage:

> "Heal the sick, cleanse the lepers, raise the dead, cast out devils" (Matthew 10:8).

as an argument for divine healing today is to violate the simplest, clearest teaching of the Word of God. Let us remind you, Jesus commanded His disciples *not* to preach this message to any but to Israel, and if it is to be applied at all, it should be given only to the nation of Israel. To give it to any other is to disregard utterly the Lord's clear command, and to wrest the Scriptures. Remember Jesus says:

"Go *not* into the way of the Gentiles. . .

But go rather to the lost sheep of the house of Israel" (Matthew 10:5-6).

THE KINGDOM MESSAGE

And then follows the message they were to bring:

"And as ye go, preach, saying, The kingdom of heaven is at hand" (Matthew 10:7).

May I ask again, sincerely, is this the message we are to bring today? Is this what we tell sinners when they come to us for salvation? Is this the message Paul gave to the Philippian jailor when he cried, "Sirs, what must I do to be saved?" Is this what you would tell a sinner today if he came seeking salvation? It was the offer of the Kingdom to Israel, and had its limited application there.

Then notice also the signs which were to accompany this Kingdom message. Jesus said:

"Heal the sick, cleanse the lepers, raise the dead, cast out devils" (Matthew 10:8).

These are Kingdom signs, apostolic gifts, which were given only to the apostles, and to those to whom they committed them during the apostolic age. These were never committed to the Church. To use this verse, therefore, from Matthew 10 as an argument for these miracles and signs today would mean that it is only for Israelites, and should include not only healings, but raising the dead and the cleansing of lepers as well. But Jesus goes on and says (and makes it even more clear):

"Provide neither gold, nor silver, nor brass in your purses.

Nor scrip for your journey, neither two coats, neither

shoes, nor yet staves: for the workman is worthy of his meat" (Matthew 10:9-10).

Is this rule practiced by those who claim that Matthew 10 is their authority for the apostolic gifts today? Remember these disciples were commanded *not* to take any offerings, or to take any money with them, to make no appeal for finances of any kind, to make no charge for their services. They were to carry only one suit of clothes, and to serve absolutely by faith, day by day. This was the commission of our Lord to His disciples. But those to whom they were sent rejected the message, and so Christ, just before He goes to the Cross, reveals to His own that the nation is to be set aside, the Kingdom postponed, the Church called out, and a new message, a brand new message, a message, not of signs and wonders, but a message of faith, is to take its place.

This was the message which God was fully to reveal after Pentecost, especially through the Apostle Paul to the Gentiles. Paul, not Peter, was to be the one to whom should be committed this great ministry. To Peter, Jesus first revealed the fact of the Church, but it remained for Paul to set forth fully the constitution, the order and the character of this Church as the Body of Christ as fully revealed in the epistles of Paul.

In future chapters we shall set forth some of these details, but now we want to emphasize in closing again, the need of "rightly dividing the Word of truth." Nothing can bring more confusion and havoc among the members of the Body of Christ, than failure to distinguish between the program of the Kingdom which still is future, and the program for the Church which is our present obligation.

Chapter Eleven

THE ONE TRUE CHURCH

THE church of Jesus Christ was a mystery hidden in the Old Testament, but fully revealed after Pentecost, by the Holy Spirit. The declaration of the Church was first made to Peter upon the occasion of his confession in Matthew 16:16. The complete revelation was committed to the Apostle Paul in particular who was peculiarly the apostle to the Gentiles, and of the Church. The apostle Peter's message, together with that of the other disciples, was peculiarly the Kingdom message, and when finally the nation rejects the offer of the Kingdom, Peter bows out of the picture, and Paul takes the stage.

Paul calls this present Church age a mystery. He explains it in Ephesians 3:1-8:

"For this cause I Paul, the prisoner of Jesus Christ for you Gentiles,

If ye have heard of the dispensation of the grace of God which is given me to you-ward:

How that by revelation he made known unto me the mystery; (as I wrote afore in few words,

Whereby, when ye read, ye may understand my knowledge in the mystery of Christ)

Which in other ages was not made known unto the sons of men, as it is now revealed unto his holy apostles and prophets by the Spirit:

That the Gentiles should be fellow-heirs, and of the

same body, and partakers of his promise in Christ by the gospel.

Whereof I was made a minister, according to the gift of the grace of God given unto me. . .that I should preach among the Gentiles the unsearchable riches of Christ."

This is the key passage in the proper understanding of the revelation of the Kingdom, and its relation to the Church. It is the key to "rightly dividing the Word of truth." Notice the following points which Paul sets forth in this remarkable passage, which every Christian who wants to understand God's program thoroughly ought to study with the greatest of care:

1. Paul's ministry was specifically to the Gentiles (verse 1).
2. It is called the Dispensation of the Grace of God (verse 2).
3. It was received by special revelation (verse 3).
4. It is called the mystery of Christ (verse 4).
5. This mystery was not revealed in other ages as it is now (verse 5).
6. Paul was God's special instrument and agent for the setting forth of this great new truth (verse 7).

THE MINISTRY OF PETER

The ministry of Peter, however, in sharp contrast, was of a different nature, for Paul did not receive his information from the other apostles, but by special revelation from God. His ministry was to be specifically to the Gentiles, while the other apostles were to minister particularly to Israel. This does not mean that Paul did not first go to the Jews, or that Peter did not go to the Gentiles, but generally speaking, the ministry of Paul was to the uncircumcision, while Peter's was to the circumcision. This is made clear in Galatians 2:6-9. After

Paul had declared that he had received his new message direct from heaven, he says this:

"But of these who seemed to be somewhat, (the disciples at Jerusalem) . . . added nothing to me:

But contrariwise, when they saw that the gospel of the uncircumcision (to the Gentiles) was committed unto me, as the gospel of the circumcision (to Israel) was unto Peter;

(For he that wrought effectually in Peter to the apostleship of the circumcision, the same was mighty in me toward the Gentiles:)

And when James, Cephas, and John, who seemed to be pillars, perceived the grace that was given unto me, they gave to me and Barnabas the right hands of fellowship; that *we should go unto the heathen, and they unto the circumcision*" (Galatians 2:6-9).

PETER'S MESSAGE

This alone will explain, I am sure, the reason for the difference in the message of Peter, and the message of Paul. Peter also recognized this new mystery, and tells us concerning this message of grace to the Church:

"Of which salvation the prophets have inquired and searched diligently, who prophesied of the grace that should come unto you:

Searching what, or what manner of time the Spirit of Christ which was in them did signify, when it testified beforehand the sufferings of Christ, and the glory that should follow.

Unto whom it was revealed, that not unto themselves, but unto us they did minister the things, which are now reported unto you by them that have preached the gospel unto you with the Holy Ghost sent down from heaven;

which things the angels desire to look into" (I Peter
1:10-12).

To the Old Testament prophet, the Church, Peter says, was
a mystery, and they inquired diligently as to the meaning. But
today the Church is a mystery no longer. We who live on this
side of Pentecost, know the truth of the Body of Christ, but
before that time it was a mystery. Of course, we recognize
that God knew this all before. He knew the nation would
reject their Messiah, and had already planned from eternity
that after His rejection He would reveal this mystery of the
Church in this dispensation. Paul tells us in Ephesians 3:11
that it was "according to the eternal purpose which he purposed
in Christ Jesus our Lord." Today then, the Kingdom is set
aside, and God is gathering from among the nations a Body
to be the Bride of Christ. When this Body is complete the
Lord will return, take His Church home, and then set up
the long promised, long-awaited millennial Kingdom upon
earth in fulfillment of all His promises.

CHURCH STILL FUTURE

When Jesus, therefore, made the revelation of the Church
to Peter, and the disciples, the Church was still future, for
He says, "Upon this rock I *will* build my church." It is not
something that will be continued, but a future thing. And
this is where so many make the mistake and stumble over the
difference between the Kingdom which is still future, and the
Church which is being called out today. It is Christ Himself
who will build the Church, and there can be only one church.

THE TRUE CHURCH

The question, therefore, arises, "If the Church was still
future, when did it begin?" We have the record in the second
chapter of Acts. There is given the record of the Holy

Spirit coming down in abiding power and presence upon one hundred and twenty disciples and forming the Church, the Body of Christ, born as an infant on Pentecost. It was still small in numbers, but complete in being, just as a new babe is small, but still complete as a child of its parents. It still needed to grow and add millions upon millions of cells, one by one, until it reaches maturity. But it was already a complete personality. Just so, the Church born on Pentecost has been growing, adding members all through these past nineteen centuries, and soon we believe the last member will be added, and she will be taken to be with the Lord, and the Kingdom age will once more begin. Whatever happened to the Church at Pentecost, therefore, happened to the complete Body of Christ, even though few in visible members.

We must remind you again that in the mind of God this body was always complete. He saw every member of that mystical body from eternity, and He had ordained them from eternity to be His own, to be added in due time to the Body. No one member will be missing bye and bye. Paul tells us in Ephesians 1:3,

> "Blessed be the God and Father of our Lord Jesus Christ, who had blessed us with all spiritual blessings in heavenly places in Christ.
>
> According as he hath chosen us in him before the foundation of the world, that we should be holy and without blame before him in love:
>
> Having predestinated us unto the adoption of children by Jesus Christ to himself, according to the good pleasure of his will,
>
> To the praise of the glory of his grace, wherein he hath made us accepted in the beloved."

These then constitute the one true Church, independent of

color, race, social standing, or denomination. God chose every member of the true church long before there were denominations and sects and divisions and organizations, and He Himself in choosing the Church ignores all these human names and differences. We recognize only one true Church. Men speak of this and that denomination as a church, but there is no Bible ground for such classification. They speak of a building as a church, but a church is not a pile of stone and brick and lumber, but a living organism. Any place where believers meet together there we have a local church containing a few members of the one true Church of Jesus Christ. Our Lord Himself gave us its description when He said in Matthew 18:20,

"Where two or three are gathered together in my name, there am I in the midst of them."

That is more than a promise; it is a fact. They may meet in a cathedral, temple, or tabernacle, in gospel hall, store building, or tent, in a room in a house, under the trees, or on a desert island, in a shack or in caves and catacombs. Whereever two or three meet in Jesus' Name, there you have a church, a part of the one true Church. The building has absolutely nothing to do with it at all. The early church had no buildings, but met in houses and homes, and oftentimes in caves and cellars because of the persecution.

It's Constitution

In this primitive church, the only creed was the Bible, the only rule for faith and practice was the Scriptures. There were no man-made confessions, creeds or articles of belief. These were all added as controversies arose, and the truth was denied, and the Church deemed it necessary to state in condensed form what it believed and stood for. The purpose of their meeting together was always to remember the Lord in the breaking of bread, to pray, to fellowship one with another, to encourage each other, to study the Word, and to receive instruction for evangelizing those outside the fellowship, and to bring them to Christ. They did not seek to make church members, but to get men saved, and then they automatically became members of the one and only true Church, the Body of Christ, and their identification with a local body for fellowship became their testimony that they belonged to the one true Church of God.

The Marks of the Church

While the various members of the body of Christ may differ in many outward respects, they all bear the same marks of the true believer. As we said, they may worship in cathedral or hovel, in gospel hall or temple, may have a highly ritualistic service, or the simplest of the simple, may wear peculiar clothing or be entirely informal. All these trifles make no difference at all, but in certain respects they are all alike. They are all born again by faith, they all believe on the Lord Jesus Christ, and His finished work, His deity and virgin birth, His atoning death and resurrection and coming again. They all have repentance toward God, and faith toward Jesus Christ, they all believe in holiness of walk and conduct, they all hate sin. They all believe in prayer and worshiping God.

The Authority of the Church

The True Church also has but one head. Christ is the Head of the Church, and the only Head.

"And he is before all things, and by him all things consist.

And he is the head of the body, the church: who is the beginning, the firstborn from the dead; that in all things he might have the preeminence" (Colossians 1: 17-18).

Jesus Christ, therefore, is both the foundation and the only Head of the one true Church. To deny this headship and to give it to any other, be he man or angel, is to deny the headship of Christ. He is both Foundation and Head, we repeat. As Foundation, He assures us of our safety and security. As Head He directs and commands and guides, for all of which we are exceedingly thankful. If our salvation were built on any other rock, particularly a human, we should despair. If our guidance and direction came from any other, even a church, we would be led astray. How thankful, therefore, we ought to be that our destiny is in the hands of our Saviour, who said:

"And I give unto them eternal life; and they shall never perish, neither shall any man pluck them out of my hand" (John 10:28).

In closing, therefore, may I ask you, my friend, are you a member of the One True Church which is the Body of Christ? Nothing else counts! The only way to be saved, the only way to become a member of that Body of Christ, the one true Church, is by believing the words of its Head, the Lord Jesus Christ, who said:

"Verily, verily, I say unto you, He that heareth my word, and believeth on him that sent me, hath everlasting life, and shall not come into condemnation; but is passed from death unto life" (John 5:24).

Chapter Twelve

THE MESSAGE OF PENTECOST

THE key to the proper understanding of the nature, character, purpose and destiny of the Church of Jesus Christ is "rightly dividing the Word of truth," and carefully distinguishing between the Kingdom and the Church. The Church is not the Kingdom, and the Kingdom is not The Church, nor ever can be. The message which John the Baptist and the disciples preached to Israel, and which Israel rejected, was not the message which Paul preached after Pentecost.

To most people, even Christians, the Church and the Kingdom mean the same thing, and so they talk about building the Kingdom and getting folks into the Kingdom. It is an error and misunderstanding of the clear teaching of the Word, for the Church is not the Kingdom nor is the Kingdom ever the Church. The Kingdom is the reign of Christ on the earth in personal presence, over the nation of Israel and through them, over the entire world.

This was the message the prophets of old preached. They told Israel that the Messiah, when He came would set up the Kingdom on the earth, which was to be a literal kingdom. This was the offer that was made to Israel at the first coming of Christ. It was, "Repent ye, for the Kingdom of heaven is at hand." John the Baptist preached it. The disciples preached it, and Jesus proclaimed it. But the nation of Israel rejected this offer of the Kingdom, and so Jesus began to reveal a truth which had never been known before. He began to show how the Kingdom would be postponed, and in the meantime, a new thing, the Church, would be formed, a mystery which had not been before revealed.

This truth was not known to the Old Testament prophets, nor to John the Baptist, nor fully to the apostles and disciples until after Pentecost. All they looked for was the setting up of the restored Kingdom of Israel upon earth, with its capitol in Jerusalem. Then after the nation rejected the Lord, He begins to make known the Church, heretofore, a mystery, hidden in God.

Rightly Dividing the Word

This truth of the mystery of the Body of Christ is the key to understanding the Scriptures, and more especially, the understanding of prophecy. As the Old Testament prophet looked ahead, he saw only the glory of the Kingdom age. The references to the suffering Messiah, and the intervening age of grace were a great mystery to him. That is why John the Baptist sent disciples to Jesus asking, "Art thou he that should come, or look we for another?" He could not understand why Jesus did not set up the Kingdom. That is why the disciples asked again and again, "Wilt thou at this time restore the Kingdom again to Israel?" For as yet they knew nothing of the Church of this present dispensation.

Even when Peter preached at Pentecost, he still addressed his message directly to Israel. It was the offer of the Kingdom given once more to the nation of Israel. This offer continued until the seventh chapter of the book of Acts. Up until the seventh of Acts the Gospel is never preached to a single Gentile. Then Stephen, the preaching deacon, having been put on trial by the Jews, delivers his great sermon, the last great offer of the Kingdom to the nation of Israel. He concludes this sermon as follows:

"Ye stiffnecked and uncircumcised in heart and ears, ye do always resist the Holy Ghost: as your fathers did, so do ye.

Which of the prophets have not your fathers persecuted? and they have slain them which shewed before of the coming of the Just One; of whom ye have been now the betrayers and murderers:

Who have received the law by the disposition of angels, and have not kept it" (Acts 7:51-53).

Only to Israel

We emphasize again that this message is still to the nation of Israel. Up until this point the message had not been given to the Gentiles at all. Stephen's entire sermon, as Peter's sermons previous to this, are addressed to Israel, and in this particular message Stephen rehearses the history of Israel, and in concluding his message lays the rejection and murder of the Messiah right at their feet.

Now notice the reaction on the part of the leaders of Israel:

"When they heard these things, they were cut to the heart, (Stephen had accused them of the murder of Jesus) and they gnashed on him with their teeth.

But he, being full of the Holy Ghost, looked up stedfastly into heaven, and saw the glory of God, and Jesus standing on the right hand of God,

And said, Behold, I see the heavens opened, and the Son of man standing on the right hand of God" (Acts 7:54-56).

Here then is the final appeal and offer to Israel. Stephen saw heaven opened, and Jesus *standing!* Notice that Jesus was not sitting. He had arisen for this particular occasion. The door of heaven was opened, (the first time since He had gone back to heaven) and their Messiah was now standing, ready to return and set up the Kingdom, *if* they would only confess their sin and receive Him as their Messiah and Lord. He saw Jesus *standing*, ready to return. When Jesus went to heaven He *sat down*, and today He is *sitting* at God's right hand. The writer of Hebrews definitely tells us:

"When he had by himself purged our sins, *sat down* on the right hand of the Majesty on high" (Hebrews 1:3).

Again in Hebrews 10, verse 12, we read the same thing:

"But this man, (Jesus) after he had offered one sacrifice for sins for ever, *sat down* on the right hand of God"

HE SAT DOWN

Jesus, therefore, was seated after His ascension, on God's right hand, until He should come back again. And now Stephen sees Him, not sitting, but *standing*. He must, therefore, have risen from His sitting position which He assumed upon His ascension. Now when we get up from our seat, we do it either to greet someone, or to go somewhere. And that, we believe is the meaning here. It is the last appeal, and Stephen says in essence, "If you will but yet accept Him, He will return, deliver Israel, set up the Kingdom, bring in the glorious, Messianic reign. Even now the door of heaven is open for Him to come, and He is standing ready to return, *if* you will but receive Him." This was the crucial moment in the history of Israel. What will the answer be? The record tells us clearly the sad, sad story:

"Then they cried out with a loud voice, and stopped their ears, and ran upon him with one accord.

And cast him out of the city, and stoned him" (Acts 7:57-58).

This was the answer of his accusers. The King is now finally rejected, and the Son of man sits down again, and heaven closes to the nation, and now the Church is to take over the spotlight. How significant, therefore, that which follows in verse 58:

> "And cast him out of the city, and stoned him: and the witnesses laid down their clothes at a young man's feet, whose name was Saul" (Acts 7:58)

ENTER PAUL

Here a new name is introduced in the narrative. A young man named Saul, later called Paul, the Apostle to the Gentiles, now comes into view. He is to be God's channel through which the great revelation of the Church, the mystery of the Body, was to be given to us. Chapter eight of the book of Acts, therefore, opens with the second mention of Saul:

> "And Saul was consenting unto his death" (Acts 8:1).

We want you to notice carefully the new program which is introduced in the eighth chapter of Acts. Up until now, we repeat, the Gospel had been preached by Peter and the apostles *only and exclusively* to the Nation of Israel. Not a Gentile had been addressed. But now, after the final rejection of the Kingdom message by Israel, God turns to Samaria:

> "Then Philip went down to the city of Samaria, and preached Christ unto them" (Acts 8:5).

Now for the first time, the message goes beyond Judaea. As a result of Stephen's death, and Saul's terrible persecution of the Church, we read:

> "Therefore they that were scattered abroad went every where preaching the word" (Acts 8:4).

Of course, all of this was according to the order which Jesus had definitely laid down:

> "Both in Jerusalem, and in all Judaea, and in Samaria" (Acts 1:8).

Jerusalem had now heard the message and rejected it. Now

comes step number two in the program of God, and the Gospel goes to Samaria. God's program, you notice, goes on, even though it takes persecution of His children to carry it out.

Then we come to Acts 9, and the conversion of the Apostle Paul, who was to be God's instrument to bring the message to the uttermost parts of the earth, in harmony with the order:

"Both in Jerusalem, and in all Judaea, and in Samaria, and unto the uttermost part of the earth" (Acts 1:8).

Then follows chapter 10, with the conversion of the Gentile Cornelius and his household. Peter to whom had been committed the keys of the Kingdom now goes to the house of Cornelius, and opens the Gospel to the Gentiles there. He had used the "keys" first when he preached to the Jews on Pentecost. Again he had used the "keys" the second time to open the Gospel to the believers in Samaria, and now comes the third and final use of the keys of the Kingdom as Peter preaches the Gospel and opens the door to the Gentiles in the home of the Gentile, Cornelius.

Now, this having been accomplished, Paul comes into the limelight, and takes over. Soon after, in Acts 13 Paul and Barnabas are sent as missionaries, and from this point on Peter disappears from the record. His work was done, and we know little or nothing about his activities or his whereabouts after that, until the day he died.

THE NEW PROMINENCE OF THE GENTILE

Israel also now passes out of the picture, and more and more the Church becomes Gentile, rather than Jewish in character. The new message takes the place of the Kingdom message, and we hear no more about "Repent ye, and be baptized; for the Kingdom of heaven is at hand." This message is now to give way to another, the message of the Gospel of grace in this dispensation. Instead, it is now "Believe on the Lord Jesus Christ, and thou shalt be saved, and thy house."

It is the message of grace that Paul was to bring together with the other apostles. While Peter had preached baptism as a condition for the Kingdom, Paul preaches baptism as an obligation and a testimony, but not a requirement for salvation. Peter had preached John's baptism. Paul preached Christian baptism, not as a means of salvation, but as a testimony of a salvation which has already been accomplished, and accepted. We are not baptized *to be* saved, but because we have *been* saved by the grace of God.

If men, therefore, would only distinguish between the Kingdom message, and the message of grace committed to us, it would end 95% of all the differences and controversies which have split the professing Church during all these past ages. We may well again call your attention to the verse in II Timothy 2:

> "Study to shew thyself approved unto God, a workman that needeth not to be ashamed, rightly dividing the word of truth" (II Timothy 2:15).

If we are to rightly divide the word of truth, we must first of all recognize that the ministry of the apostles, after Pentecost up until the seventh chapter of Acts, was exclusively to Israel, and limited to Jerusalem and Judaea. This was in perfect harmony with the Kingdom message which Christ gave in Matthew 10, where He said that they were to go only to the lost sheep of the house of Israel, and to preach "the Kingdom of heaven is at hand," and to confirm it with signs and miracles of the Kingdom message. Peter preached only to Jews at Pentecost. How clearly this is stated in Acts 2:5,

"And there were dwelling at Jerusalem Jews, devout men, out of every nation under heaven" (Acts 2:5).

They were all Jews, from every country. These had come from all over the world to be present at the feast, and they were all of the nation of Israel. In verses 9 to 11 we are told:

"Parthians, and Medes, and Elamites, and the dwellers in Mesopotamia, and in Judaea, and Cappadocia, in Pontus, and Asia,

Phrygia, and Pamphylia, in Egypt, and in the parts of Libya about Cyrene, and strangers of Rome, Jews and proselytes" (Acts 2:9-10).

They were Jews and proselytes, Gentiles who had become Jews by accepting their religion and their circumcision. Had this company accepted the message as a nation they would have been prepared and ready, knowing as they did the language of every people and tongue, to go out immediately, and proclaim the message and bring in the glorious Messianic age which the Lord has promised. But they rejected the message, and now the fulfillment of this must wait until after the Church is gone, and the hundred and forty-four thousand of Revelation 7 are raised up under similar circumstances to carry out the program which was offered to Israel at Pentecost, but was rejected by them. In future chapters we shall develop more fully this most important truth upon which hinges our proper understanding of the program of God in this dispensation and the one to come.

Chapter Thirteen

UPON THIS ROCK

When Jesus came into the coasts of Caesarea Philippi he asked his disciples, saying, Whom do men say that I the Son of man am?
And Simon Peter answered and said, Thou art the Christ, the Son of the living God.
And Jesus answered and said unto him, Blessed art thou, Simon Bar-jona; for flesh and blood hath not revealed it unto thee, but my Father which is in heaven.
And I say unto thee, that thou art Peter, and upon this rock I will build my church; and the gates of hell shall not prevail against it.

Matthew 16:13, 16-18

IN this most important passage from Matthew 16 we have the first mention of the Church in the entire Scriptures. The word never occurs in the Bible until we reach this chapter. In Matthew the King had come to offer the Kingdom to Israel, and had sent John the Baptist and His disciples forth with the message, "Repent ye, for the kingdom of heaven is at hand." But the offer had been rejected by the nation, and now the Lord begins to reveal a new thing, not known heretofore; namely, that during the time of the rejection of the King, He would do a new thing, build a Church, against which the gates of hell could not prevail. This Church is called in Scripture His Body.

Now when the Lord made this announcement in Matthew

16, the Church did not as yet exist, but was future, and so He said:

> "Upon this rock I will build my church" (Matthew 16:18).

To begin a building we must first lay the foundation, and so in this first mention of the Church, about which the Lord does not give the details, we have Christ merely revealing the foundation of this new thing which was to be more definitely revealed later and elaborated upon by the Apostle Paul and the other apostles. We shall see that this building consists of lively stones and that the vessels in this building represent those who belong to the Lord Jesus Christ. And so our Lord says:

> "Thou art Peter, and upon this rock I will build my church."

Untold confusion has reigned in the hearts of many Bible students and believers over the interpretation of this particular passage, "Thou art Peter, and upon this rock I will build my church." Many and varied indeed have been the views set forth by expositors, each interpreter claiming that he was right, and basing his theories upon the Scriptures.

In general, there are three views among professing Christendom setting forth the interpretation of this "rock."

1. First, there are those who tell us that the confession of Peter, "Thou art the Christ, the Son of the living God," is the foundation stone, and therefore, all who confess this are saved and become a part of the church, and members of His Body.

2. Second, there are those who teach that Peter himself was the Rock referred to in this particular verse, so that when Jesus said, "Thou art Peter, and upon this rock I will build my church," He was teaching that the Church is

built upon the Apostle Peter, as a person. This is the general teaching of the Catholic Church, which also teaches that Peter was the first Pope, and that he resided for a period of time before his death in the city of Rome.

3. The third group holds that the Rock in this verse is none other than the Lord Jesus Christ Himself. He was the foundation and the cornerstone of the building, and, therefore, those who confess Him, repent of their sins, and trust Him, are built upon the foundation, Jesus Christ.

Who is Right

There are other interpretations and variations of these interpretations, but these are the ones generally held by professing Christendom. Now, before trying to establish which one of these is the Scriptural interpretation in our opinion, we must face the fact that sincere and earnest and able Bible scholars are found among these different groups, men who are honest and well-meaning in their opinion. We are not judging any of them, we are merely turning to the Word of God to find out what we believe to be the correct interpretation. What we have to say, therefore, concerning the passage on Peter and the Rock, is not in any sense to set ourselves up to judge others who do not agree, or to antagonize those who hold other views, but only that we may as sincere followers of the Lord seek to know what His Word teaches. And so with this motive clearly before us, we shall in love point out where we believe the error lies, and what the Bible clearly teaches.

Who is the Foundation?

There are many passages of inspired Scripture which deal with the subject. In I Corinthians chapter 10 Paul tells us definitely that the Rock was "Christ." He is there, of course, referring to the rock in the wilderness which was smitten by

Moses, that beautiful type of the Lord Jesus on the Cross of Calvary, and tells us that typically and in shadow this rock represented the Lord Jesus Christ.

Then again in I Corinthians 3, verses 9 to 11, Paul tells us as follows:

> "For we are labourers together with God: ye are God's husbandry, ye are God's building.
>
> According to the grace of God which is given unto me, as a wise masterbuilder, I have laid the foundation, and another buildeth thereon. But let every man take heed how he buildeth thereupon.
>
> For other foundation can no man lay than that is laid, *which is Jesus Christ"* (I Corinthians 3:9-11).

Now you will notice that Paul says in this passage clearly and unmistakably, "Jesus Christ is the foundation stone upon which the Church is builded." He compares the Church to a building. A building has not only a foundation, but also a superstructure. The foundation and the superstructure are connected and united in one great building. If you have watched a building go up, you will have noticed that after the foundation is laid, the builder lays upon this foundation the sill, and fastens it to the foundation. Then upon this sill, the superstructure is secured. Now this sill becomes part of the foundation and the superstructure both. It binds the two together in one. The apostles and the prophets, including Peter, are this binder standing between the foundation and the house, and therefore, are classed both with the foundation and with the house. I am sure that this will explain the passage from Ephesians 2 which has troubled many.

> "Now therefore ye are no more strangers and foreigners, but fellowcitizens with the saints, and of the household of God;

And are built upon the foundation of the apostles and prophets, Jesus Christ himself being the chief cornerstone,

In whom all the building fitly framed together groweth unto an holy temple in the Lord:

In whom ye also are builded together for an habitation of God through the Spirit" (Ephesians 2:19-22).

You will notice that the apostles and the prophets are called the foundation with Christ as the cornerstone. It does not say that Peter alone is the foundation, but it includes the apostles and the prophets of the Old Testament.

EXPLANATION

How are we going to understand this particular passage? It was through the apostles and the prophets that God gave us the revelation of His program, both of the Kingdom and the Church, and therefore, it is upon the foundation of this revelation that we build our hope of eternal life. But all of this was built upon the Person of the Lord Jesus who is the true foundation. Now while these apostles and prophets are the intervening link between Christ and us in the sense that they have given us the revelation in the Scripture, they become a part both of the foundation and of the building.

Peter, to whom the Lord spake the new revelation of the Church, knew very well that he was not *the* rock, but only a part of the building. Peter himself *never* claimed that *he* was the rock upon which the Church was to be built. And if we want to know the real interpretation of Christ's words, "Upon this rock I will build my church," we can do no better than to go to the Apostle Peter himself. Certainly if he understood it in this way, he would tell us definitely. Listen to what he has to say in I Peter 2:1-6,

"Wherefore laying aside all malice, and all guile, and hypocrisies, and envies, and all evil speakings,

As newborn babes, desire the sincere milk of the word, that ye may grow thereby:

If so be ye have tasted that the Lord is gracious.

To whom coming, as unto a living stone, disallowed indeed of men, but chosen of God, and precious,

Ye also, as lively stones, are built up a spiritual house, an holy priesthood, to offer up spiritual sacrifices, acceptable to God by Jesus Christ.

Wherefore also it is contained in the scripture, Behold, I lay in Sion a chief corner stone, elect, precious: and he that believeth on him shall not be confounded."

Peter tells us in no uncertain language that the rock on which the Church of Jesus Christ is builded is none other than our Lord.

PETROS AND PETRA

Now with these Scriptures in mind, will you turn to the passage in Matthew 16.

"And I say also unto thee, That thou art Peter, and upon this rock I will build my church; and the gates of hell shall not prevail against it" (Matthew 16:18).

It is unfortunate that the translators of our English Bible have left some words in this verse untranslated. The word "Peter" used here, is *"Petros"* in the Greek, and means "a little stone," but the word translated "rock" in this same verse is *"Petra"* in the Greek, and means "a large rock." The word, "Petros," in Matthew 16 is the diminutive of "Petra." If we were, therefore, to translate these words, we would have this:

"Thou art a little stone, Peter, but upon this big *rock* I will build my church."

Another characteristic of the passage is that before the word, *Petra,* (big stone) the definite article is used, indicating that there is only one. But before the word, *Petros* (the little stone), no article is used, indicating that Peter was not the only pebble, but that he was one of many, many others. The rock then was Christ. He is the Rock upon which the Church is built, and we as living stones according to His own testimony are built upon this Rock.

Peter's Testimony

We see from this that Peter did not claim that he was the rock on which the church was to be built, but instead, he was the first one to admit that he, with us and all believers, was a little stone in the building of the church, upon the one foundation, Jesus Christ. That is why he says:

> "To whom coming, as unto a living stone, disallowed indeed of men, but chosen of God, and precious" (I Peter 2:4).

In this passage Peter calls Jesus a living stone, and significantly the word used in the Greek is *lithon*, and means "a large rock" in the singular. And then he continues in I Peter 2:5,

> "Ye also, as lively stones, are built up a spiritual house."

In this verse the word, "stones," is in the plural, and is the translation of the word, *lithoi*, indicating that there are many. Christ then, according to Peter, is the *lithon*, *one* foundation Rock, and we are the *lithoi*, the many living stones built upon the foundation into the building, Jesus Christ, and His Church.

Here then we have the complete picture given in the Scriptures. Among the many, many figures of the Church, Peter uses that of a house. Christ is the foundation and the cornerstone. To build upon any other foundation is to build upon sinking sand. Our Lord Himself warns us about building upon any other foundation than the one foundation Rock. To

place our hope and our trust in anyone else than the Lord
Jesus Christ for our salvation is to build upon sinking sand.
We repeat again the verse which everyone ought to meditate
upon frequently:

"Neither is there salvation in any other: for there is
none other name under heaven given among men, whereby we must be saved" (Acts 4:12).

The question, therefore, comes: on what foundation are
you building your hope for eternity? All men are builders,
but the first essential is the foundation, for without it all the
superstructure can mean nothing. And Christ is the only
foundation for our hope of eternal life. If we are building
on the sand of human philosophy and works, it makes no
difference how beautiful we may build, it must perish. You
may build a moral, educated, cultured and philanthropic house,
but when the storms of judgment come, it will not stand,
for then only the foundation will count.

So we conclude this chapter by asking, where are you
building? Upon what are you resting? Are you resting on the
fact that you are a moral, religious, cultured, honest, sincere
and law-abiding citizen? All of that is fine, and everyone
ought to be all of these things, but if we have not received
Jesus Christ as our personal Saviour, we are still building upon
a foundation which shall not withstand the storms of the
judgment of God. But, if you have come as a poor, lost,
unworthy sinner to the foot of the Cross, and repented of your
sins, and believed on the Lord Jesus Christ who is the only
foundation, then you are safe and secure for all eternity, and
then all these other good things will abide. What are you
building on today? Have you personally come to Christ as a
poor, lost sinner and by faith received Him as your only hope
and salvation?

Chapter Fourteen

THE KEYS OF THE KINGDOM

*And I will give unto thee the keys of the kingdom of
heaven: and whatsoever thou shalt bind on earth shall be
bound in heaven: and whatsoever thou shalt loose on earth
shall be loosed in heaven.*

Matthew 16:19

THESE words, significant and important, yet so much misunderstood, were spoken to the Apostle Peter on the occasion
of his confession in Matthew 16:

"Thou art the Christ, the Son of the living God"
(Matthew 16:16).

After the Lord had announced that upon the one foundation, the Rock, Christ, the Church should be built, He next
addresses Peter and commits to him the keys of the Kingdom
of Heaven. We have pointed out previously that Christ is
the foundation stone on which the church was to be built,
and He is also the Door into the Body of Christ, and Peter
and all the rest of the believers in all ages were stones built
upon this foundation. But what is meant by the "keys of the
kingdom of heaven"? Notice carefully that Jesus does not
give unto Peter the keys to the Church, but He gives unto
him the keys of the "kingdom of heaven." It is very important
that we note this distinction with extreme care. The Church
consists of that body of born again believers who by faith
in the Lord Jesus Christ have become members of His Body,

the one true Church. The "Kingdom of Heaven" refers to
the sphere of Christian profession, and deals with professing
Christendom, as set forth by Jesus in Matthew 13, in the
parables of the Kingdom. This is referred to as the "mystery"
of the Kingdom of Heaven, while the Kingdom itself will be
established upon the return of Christ.

Various Interpretations

With this distinction in mind, look at some of the interpretations of this difficult passage. There is a large group in
professing Christendom who teach that Jesus gave to Peter
as a person the full authority as head of the Church to open
and shut heaven to men and to forgive sins. This authority,
it is taught, was handed down by apostolic succession to the
bishops and the priests and the officers of the church. In
connection with these verses they quote Matthew 18:18,

> "Whatsoever ye shall bind on earth shall be bound in
> heaven: and whatsoever ye shall loose on earth shall be
> loosed in heaven."

There is still one more Scripture which is usually linked
with these, and we want to take all three of them together.
This one is found in John 20:23.

> "Whose soever sins ye remit, they are remitted unto
> them; and whose soever sins ye retain, they are retained."

On these Scriptures is based the authority for men to forgive sins. We shall take these up one by one as we go along.

Second Interpretation

There is a second group who claim that the keys of the
kingdom were given to Peter, and through Peter to the
constituted officers of the church, the elders and the bishops
and the pastors, so that when they excommunicate a person

from the local assembly, he is shut out by this act from heaven, and only as they admit him can he re-enter again.

There is still another group which teaches that the "keys of the Kingdom" constitute the preaching of the Gospel. When we faithfully preach the Word, then we either open or shut the door to those who hear the Word. Those who hear the Word, and believe what we are preaching, will, of course, be saved, and heaven is opened up unto them, but if they reject, they remain lost, and so heaven is closed to them. In this respect, all who preach the Gospel, therefore, have the keys of the kingdom of heaven, and through their word, whether accepted or rejected, they are the ones who open or shut the door of salvation.

Now while we believe that this is the meaning of the verse, "whose soever sins ye remit, they are remitted," we do not believe that the same thing holds true for the "keys of the kingdom of heaven." The book of Acts gives us the answer, we believe, to the proper interpretation of this vexing question. There are at least three keys which are mentioned in the book of Acts and committed to Peter.

Opening the Door to the Jews

The first use of the keys was at Pentecost. Here Peter was God's chosen vessel to present the Gospel first to the Jewish nation. He opened the door of opportunity to Israel, according to God's divine order, "Beginning at Jerusalem." The second use of the keys came in Acts chapter 8. Following the death of Stephen and the persecution which arose, Philip, the preaching deacon, had gone to Samaria and witnessed a great revival. Before this preaching to the Samaritans could become official, however, Peter must use the keys committed to him.

"Now when the apostles which were at Jerusalem heard

that Samaria had received the word of God, they sent unto them Peter and John" (Acts 8:14).

The question arises, Why did they send Peter and John to the city of Samaria? It was simply because Peter had committed to him the keys to open the Gospel to Samaria after he had used them the first time in Jerusalem to the Jews. Beginning in Jerusalem and then in Samaria was God's divine order. For while these Samaritans believed, nothing had as yet happened to establish their part in Pentecostal power. That could only be opened by the bearer of the keys, Peter himself. Verses 15, 16 and 17 make this very clear:

"Who, when they were come down, prayed for them, that they might receive the Holy Ghost:

(For as yet he was fallen upon none of them: only they were baptized in the name of the Lord Jesus.)

Then laid they their hands on them, and they received the Holy Ghost" (Acts 8:15-17).

Now this was Peter's second use of the keys of the Kingdom of Heaven, to open up the message to the Samaritans. But one more is to follow in harmony with Christ's order: beginning at Jerusalem, and in all Judaea, and in Samaria, and unto the uttermost part of the earth. This record we find in Acts 10. In Acts chapter 7 Israel rejects the final message through Stephen. In the eighth chapter the message goes to Samaria; in the ninth chapter Saul is converted to prepare him for the message which was to go through him to all the world, and is introduced after the final use of the keys by Peter which occurs in Acts 10. In this chapter (Acts 10), Peter sees a vision of a great sheet let down from heaven containing all manner of four-footed beasts of the earth, and wild beasts, and creeping things, and fowls of the air, and Peter was commanded to eat. But Peter was a Jew, and a

Jew was not allowed to eat unclean foods forbidden by the law. Thus Peter made strenuous objection and said:

"Not so, Lord; for I have never eaten anything that is common or unclean" (Acts 10:14).

But the answer comes from heaven again to Peter:

"What God hath cleansed, that call not thou common" (Acts 10:15).

Now all of this, of course, was to prepare Peter for the third use of the keys. Peter was a Jew, and, therefore, could legally have no dealings with the Gentiles. They were unclean to him. But while all this was going on, a group of messengers sent by the Gentile Cornelius in Caesarea was approaching Peter's house in Joppa to ask him to come to Caesarea and open the door of the Gospel to them. Peter would undoubtedly have refused to go, for he knew not as yet the full truth, that the difference between the Jew and Gentile had been put away by the Cross of Calvary, the middle wall of partition had been broken down between Jew and Gentile, and he could now freely go and use the keys in the household of Cornelius. And so we read:

"Now while Peter doubted in himself what this vision which he had seen should mean, behold, the men which were sent from Cornelius had made enquiry for Simon's house, and stood before the gate.

And called, and asked whether Simon, which was surnamed Peter, were lodged there" (Acts 10: 17-18).

Then we find that the Spirit addresses Peter, and reassures him, and says:

"Arise therefore, and get thee down, and go with them, doubting nothing: for I have sent them" (Acts 10:20).

The next day they departed to Caesarea, and Cornelius was

waiting for Peter. Now will you notice carefully a very important verse which we cannot afford to overlook.

"And as Peter was coming in, Cornelius met him, and fell down at his feet, and worshiped him.

But Peter took him up, saying, Stand up; I myself also am a man" (Acts 10:25-26).

STAND UP

Peter was horrified to have this man think that he deserved any worship. Peter would permit no one to kneel to him, to fall at his feet, or to worship him. Peter made no claim to any authority that belonged to God. He refused to receive honor from men, but cried out in consternation, "*Stand up, for I also am a man.*" Peter insisted that he was only a servant of the Lord, no better than anyone else.

We have another example of this same thing in the fourth chapter of Acts. After Peter had healed the lame man at the gate called Beautiful, he had preached a stirring sermon to the crowd which assembled. But the rulers were frantic and brought Peter before the high priest, and demanded by what power he had performed this miracle. And Peter answers them. He claims absolutely no credit, he does not tell them that he is the Rock, and that he has the authority in himself, and therefore has the keys to the kingdom to admit men and women in or out of heaven. Ah, no! Far from it. Listen to the answer of Peter:

"Then Peter, filled with the Holy Ghost, said unto them, Ye rulers of the people, and elders of Israel,

If we this day be examined of the good deed done to the impotent man, by what means he is made whole:

Be it known unto you all, and to all the people of Israel, that by the name of Jesus Christ of Nazareth, whom ye crucified, whom God raised from the dead, even by him doth this man stand before you whole.

This is the stone which was set at nought of you builders, which is become the head of the corner" (Acts 4:8-11).

Notice carefully the words of Peter. He says, I am *not* the Rock. I am not the one who did this, but Christ. Peter made no claim to be able to open or shut heaven, but adds,

"Neither is there salvation in any other: for there is none other name under heaven given among men, whereby we must be saved" (Acts 4:12).

The Last Use of the Keys

Now to return to the household of Cornelius. Peter, after assuring Cornelius that he was but a man like himself, and refusing worship of any kind, preached the Gospel and:

"While Peter yet spake these words, the Holy Ghost fell on all them which heard the word.

And they of the circumcision which believed (those who had accompanied Peter from Joppa) were astonished, as many as came with Peter, because that on the Gentiles also was poured out the gift of the Holy Ghost" (Acts 10:44-45).

This was the last use of the keys committed to Peter. The door had now been opened by Peter in Jerusalem, in Samaria, and now to the Gentiles. His mission of the keys is finished, and Peter disappears from the record and Paul takes his place.

So the promise that God had given to Peter that he would be given the keys to the Kingdom had been fulfilled, and Peter had fulfilled the trust which had been committed unto him, and now the Gospel was ready to go into all the world.

Chapter Fifteen

BINDING AND LOOSING

*Verily I say unto you, Whatsoever ye shall bind on earth
shall be bound in heaven: and whatsoever ye shall loose on
earth shall be loosed in heaven"*

Matthew 18:18.

THIS is the verse which is generally quoted in connection
with Matthew 16:19 which we have already studied, where
Jesus says to Peter:

"And I will give unto thee the keys of the kingdom of
heaven."

However, the two commissions are quite distinct. The
commission of the "keys" was given to Peter alone as an individual, and was fulfilled when he had opened the door of
the Gospel, first in Jerusalem, then in Samaria, and then in
Caesarea. Then Peter's ministry was about ended, and we
know little or nothing about him from there on, except that
which he tells us in his two epistles.

The verse in Matthew concerning the binding and loosing
of things on earth and heaven, however, was given not to
Peter alone, but to the Church as a body and as a whole.
The Lord is careful not to give this authority to any one
individual, realizing the tremendous dangers which would be
involved. The setting of this verse, therefore, will make this
clear.

"Moreover if thy brother shall trespass against thee,

go and tell him his fault between thee and him alone: if he shall hear thee, thou hast gained thy brother.

But if he will not hear thee, then take with thee one or two more, that in the mouth of two or three witnesses every word may be established.

And if he shall neglect to hear them, tell it unto the church: but if he neglect to hear the church, let him be unto thee as an heathen man and a publican" (Matthew 18:15-17).

And then there follows the verse:

"Verily I say unto you, Whatsoever ye shall bind on earth shall be bound in heaven" (Matthew 18:18).

Taken in its context, therefore, you will notice that this binding and this loosing power is the prerogative of the Church, and not the work of any one individual. It deals with the discipline of an erring brother, not with the matter of salvation. The innocent victim of another's sin is to go to the guilty party first to seek to bring him to repentance. We have no right to bring a charge against any brother, to talk about a brother, to discuss something we know about a brother, until we have first gone to him alone, in private, and made an honest effort to correct him before we open our mouth to anyone else. Oh, if this rule could only be practiced among believers, what a difference it would make! But instead, we often expect the guilty party to come to us, but our Lord Jesus says:

"If thy brother shall trespass against *thee,* (you) go and tell him."

Having gone to him alone, and failing to bring him to repentance, you are not even then to blaze it abroad, but quietly take two or three others along and try it again. If this fails, then you are to bring it before the church, and it is made public. It does not say before the elders or the deacons, or the church board, but *the Church*. If he remains rebellious, he is to be disciplined, and denied all fellowship until he repents. It is in this setting, therefore, that Jesus says:

"Whatsoever ye shall bind on earth shall be bound in heaven: and whatsoever ye shall loose on earth shall be loosed in heaven."

This then is the business and the prerogative of the Church as a Body, not of Peter or an elder or any other individual official. But this authority is only valid when these Scriptural steps have been taken and followed as outlined by the Lord Jesus Christ.

THE THIRD CASE

There is one more passage which is always used in connection with Peter's use of the keys. It is John 20:23. The occasion is the first Easter evening, and the disciples were huddled together in great fear, when suddenly Jesus, their resurrected Lord, stood in their midst, and said unto them:

"Peace be unto you.

And when he had so said, he shewed unto them his hands and his side. Then were the disciples glad, when they saw the Lord.

Then said Jesus to them again, Peace be unto you: as my Father hath sent me, even so send I you.

And when he had said this, he breathed on them, and saith unto them, Receive ye the Holy Ghost:

Whose soever sins ye remit, they are remitted unto them; and whose soever sins ye retain, they are retained" (John 20:19-23).

A GENERAL COMMISSION

Now will you notice carefully in the setting of this passage that Jesus had just repeated the promise of the Holy Spirit which was to be fulfilled on the day of Pentecost? And then, after repeating this promise follows the statement, "Whose soever sins ye remit, they are remitted." It was connected with the ministry of the Holy Spirit and the preaching of the Gospel of the Lord Jesus. It was not given to Peter alone, but to all the disciples who were present.

Now this power of remitting and retaining sins, was shared by all the other disciples and those upon whom the Holy Spirit came. It involved the determination of the eternal destiny of men and women through the ministry of the disciples, but it is nowhere hinted, even remotely, that this was either the power or the authority to forgive sins, a power which belongs only to God.

PAUL EXPLAINS

Now the meaning of this commission becomes quite evident when we remember that our Lord was commissioning His disciples to go into all the world to preach the Gospel to every creature. As they preached this Gospel, they became the means for the remission of sins to those who believed, and the retaining of sins to those who rejected the message of salvation. Paul clarifies the matter in II Corinthians 2:15 when in speaking of those who preach the Gospel of Christ, he says:

> "For we are unto God a sweet savour of Christ, in them that are saved, and in them that perish:
>
> To the one we are the savour of death unto death, and to the other a savour of life unto life" (II Corinthians 2:15-16).

Here then is a passage which answers the matter fully. All who preach the Gospel become one of two things to all who listen. To those who believe the gospel which we preach, we are a savour of life unto life; to those who reject it, we

are a savour of death unto death. Those who believe the
message of salvation which we faithfully preach have their sins
remitted and forgiven, not by us, but by the Lord. Those who
refuse the message have their sins retained and are lost, not
by us, but by the Lord. The message which we preach is
not only a message of salvation to those who believe, but a
message of damnation to all those who reject.

THIS IS THE POWER

This then is the power to remit sins, or to retain them.
It is the Gospel, the message we preach, which makes us
God's messengers in offering the forgiveness of sins, and the
instrument in God's hands by which sins are remitted. Christ
gave to all who preach the Gospel the power to remit sins.
I have that power, and I exercise it every time I preach, and
offer salvation to sinners. If those who hear me believe on the
Lord Jesus Christ, and accept Him as their Lord and Saviour,
then I have been the means for the remission of their sins,
in the sense of having been God's instrument in giving them
the Word. This is the meaning of Jesus' words,

> "Whose soever sins ye remit, they are remitted unto
> them; and whose soever sins ye retain, they are retained"
> (John 20:23).

It certainly makes one tremble to think of the tremendous
responsibility that is ours everytime we get up to proclaim
the message of God's wonderful grace. To think that we
with Paul are not only a savour of life unto life, but a
savour of death unto death. No wonder Paul concludes with
the words:

> "And who is sufficient for these things?" (II Corin-
> thians. 2:16b).

A Two-Edged Sword

The word we preach, therefore, and which you hear will be your judge in the day of judgment. If you have heard the message, you are responsible for what you do with it from there on. You will have no excuse to offer in the day of judgment. The offer is to you now to accept or to reject. The writer of Hebrews says in Hebrews 4:12,

"For the word of God is quick, and powerful, and sharper than any two-edged sword."

The Word of God has two edges, one to slay sin and the other to slay the sinner. Either you believe and allow the Word of God to cleanse you and cut you loose from judgment, or that same Word which offers you salvation will be your judge in that day, and demand your eternal damnation. Jesus makes a remarkable statement in John 5:45 when He says to the Jews:

"Do not think that I will accuse you to the Father: there is one that accuseth you, even Moses, in whom ye trust.

For had ye believed Moses, ye would have believed me: for he wrote of me."

Or listen to Jesus in John 12:47,

"And if any man hear my words, and believe not, I *judge him not*: for I came not to judge the world, but to save the world.

He that rejecteth me, and receiveth not my words, hath one that judgeth him: the word that I have spoken, the same shall judge him in the last day."

Whatever God is going to do with the poor heathen who never have heard the Word we can leave with a righteous, just and merciful God, but certainly for those who have heard the Word of God there can be no excuse. You will finally be judged by one thing only — what have you done with the message of the offer of salvation being given to you even now? If you will believe today, then I have been God's channel unto salvation, so that

"Whose soever sins ye remit, they shall be remitted."

I, therefore, have the authority, the same authority Jesus gave to His disciples and to all other believers called to preach the Gospel of redeeming grace, to confidently offer eternal life to all who will believe the promises of God's Word:

"Whosoever shall call upon the name of the Lord shall be saved" (Romans 10:13).

PERSONAL RESPONSIBILITY

While all those who preach the Word become the channels through which men and women are saved, and therefore, the means in God's hands by which they receive remission of sins, it still is a personal responsibility. Everyone must decide for himself.

Here is God's promise: Jesus Christ, the Son of God, died on the Cross to save you. He arose from the grave to justify; He sent His Holy Spirit to give power to believe. He gave His Word so that all might know, and then sent messengers to faithfully proclaim this message of redemption. If you believe, then the word that we have set forth is truly the savour of life unto life for you, and your sins are remitted, and you may know that you have been forgiven. But if you reject the message, then we become a savour of death unto death, even unto you, and your sins will be retained, for:

"He that believeth on him is not condemned: but he that believeth not is condemned already, because he hath not believed in the name of the only begotten Son of God" (John 3:18).

Chapter Sixteen

THE GRACE OF GOD

*For by grace are ye saved through faith: and that not of
yourselves: it is the gift of God:*
Not of works, lest any man should boast.
*For we are his workmanship, created in Christ Jesus unto
good works, which God hath before ordained that we should
walk in them.*

Ephesians 2:8-10

THERE is one great, tremendous and important truth revealed
in the Bible which will take an eternity to appreciate and to
understand. It is the marvelous, matchless revelation of the
grace of God toward the most unworthy and hell-deserving
sinners. It is small wonder, therefore, that Satan would rob
us of the blessing of the truth of grace by adding to it all
sorts of human works, human merit and the feeble efforts
of man. I have preached the truth of grace for the past thirty
years, but I must confess that the longer I preach, the more
I realize that the truth of grace is inexhaustible, incomprehensible and beyond all human understanding.

What is Grace

Men have tried and tried to formulate a definition of grace,
but have never been able to put in human language a definition which fully expresses all that which is contained in
the term, "grace." Like electricity, light and life, we know
only what it does, rather than what it is. Why God should

choose the meanest, basest, most unworthy individuals with absolutely nothing to commend them at all to God, except their miserable, lost condition, and then exalt them to become the sons of God, members of the divine family, and use them for His glory, is beyond all reason and human understanding. Yet that is grace.

David the King

As an example of the grace of God, think for a moment of David, the king of Israel. There certainly was nothing in David to commend him to the Almighty. What a sad, sordid, disappointing record is the account of David's life. He stole another man's wife, committed deliberate adultery, and then to cover up his rotten sin he lied and finally committed a dastardly murder, and yet—and yet—God chose this man to be king of Israel, the type of the reign of Christ, and used him to give us the most sublime, heaven-breathed poetry in all the world, the book of the Psalms, and called him the "man after God's own heart."

And Peter Also

Or take the case of Simon Peter, the subject of this book. One could hardly choose a man more unfit to become the leader of the apostles, the preacher of Pentecost, the man entrusted with the keys of the Kingdom of Heaven, than Simon Peter.

What in the world did Jesus see in Simon Peter to cause him to be called to this exalted position among the disciples and the early church? Absolutely nothing. Absolutely nothing at all, and that is why He chose him, for it must be all the grace of God. God will share His glory with none else, for it must all be by grace, or it is not grace at all. I believe that is what Paul means when he tells us in I Corinthians 1:

"For ye see your calling, brethren, how that not many

wise men after the flesh, not many mighty, not many noble, are called:

But God hath chosen the foolish things of the world to confound the wise; and God hath chosen the weak things of the world to confound the things which are mighty;

And base things of the world, and things which are despised, hath God chosen, yea, and things which are not, to bring to nought things that are:

That no flesh should glory in His presence.

But of him are ye in Christ Jesus, who of God is made unto us wisdom, and righteousness, and sanctification, and redemption:

That, according as it is written, *He that glorieth, let him glory in the Lord"* (I Corinthians 1:26-31).

Notice the expression, "that no flesh should glory in his presence." Ah, yes, that's it. That's it! Only thus can we account for the fact that God chose a David, a Simon, and you and me. Certainly not because we were better than others, but in spite of the fact that we were just as bad, and probably worse. It is grace, wholly apart from our own worth or works, or merit.

Grace then becomes a most humbling truth. It leaves no place for pride. It lays us low and slays all boasting. It insists that we are utterly worthless and helpless and our only hope lies outside ourselves in Christ. Grace and pride are absolute strangers to one another.

Simon Peter had to learn this bitter lesson, and it took him most of his life to learn it, and at the very end, his parting admonition is:

"But grow in *grace,* and in the knowledge of our

Lord and Saviour Jesus Christ. To Him be glory both now and forever" (II Peter 3:18).

The best definition of grace I have ever found in the entire Scriptures is in I Samuel 2:8. It is part of the song of gratitude and praise, which Hannah voiced when her prayer for a child was answered, and Samuel had been born. In this verse Hannah says:

"The Lord killeth, and maketh alive: he bringeth down to the grave, and bringeth up.

The Lord maketh poor, and maketh rich: he bringeth low, and lifteth up" (I Samuel 2:6-7).

Now before reading the next verse, which is the definition of grace, will you notice that God is sovereign, doing just as He pleases? He needs to give an account to no man. He is the Potter, and we are the clay. He killeth and He maketh alive, as He chooses. He maketh poor, and maketh rich, according to His own purpose. God is sovereign, and until we admit this, we cannot understand the truth of grace. He is sovereign in His choice of those whom He chooses, and His choice is final, His verdict must be absolute.

There is a great deal more here, however. Before God makes alive, He first kills. Before He makes rich, He makes poor. Before we can be the recipients of the grace of eternal life, we must be slain first of all, we must be killed, and completely abandon self. We must admit our total unworthiness, and flee only to Him for grace. We must first become poor, penniless, broke, bankrupt and realize that our only salvation is the grace of God, and that we have absolutely nothing, not one farthing to offer Him in payment for salvation. How wonderfully this is expressed by the late Dr. James M. Gray, former President of the Moody Bible Institute, in that hymn which we love so much:

Nought have I gotten but what I received,
Grace hath bestowed it since I have believed.
Boasting excluded, Pride I abase,
I'm only a sinner saved by grace.

THE DEFINITION

Now we come to Hannah's definition of the grace of God in I Samuel 2:8,

"He raiseth up the poor out of the dust, and lifteth up the beggar from the dunghill, to set them among princes, and to make them inherit the throne of glory."

What a tremendous picture of grace this is! He raiseth up the poor out of the dust. Now the word translated "poor" means "empty, absolutely void, bankrupt, with no assets, but only liabilities." It excludes every possibility of helping yourself. These, and only these, He raiseth out of the dust. And then Hannah adds: "and lifteth up the beggar from the dunghill." The word for beggar, "*ebyown,*" means "destitute." The word, "dunghill," is the polite translation of the Hebrew word, "shefohth," and means literally "a garbage dump," a place where refuse and scraps are thrown, and worthless things are deposited. Now do you see that figure? The sinner is represented as sitting in the garbage dump seeking something to satisfy his hunger and his craving. One can see the picture in any city of any size by just a walk through skid row, and its alleys.

Some time ago on my way to Colorado, I stopped off to visit my son, Marvin, on Chicago's north side. After parking my car I took a short cut to the apartment, through one of Chicago's north side alleys, and there in the alley, amid the dust and the refuse and the filth and rats, I encountered one of the most pathetic sights I have ever beheld in all my life.

There beside a leaking barrel filled with garbage, and black with flies, stood one of society's outcasts, a man about sixty-five years old. Only the rim of his tattered hat was left, his shoes were tied on with rope, his coat in shreds, his trousers in tatters, his hands black with filth, his hair matted together, his beard even worse. I watched him as he pawed about in the garbage, pulled out a whiskey bottle with a teaspoon of its poison left, and lifted it to his lips. He found another drop or two in another bottle, and then he fished out a crust of garbage-sodden bread and placed it in his mouth with his filthy hands. As I stood there, I caught myself involuntarily repeating:

"He raiseth up the poor out of the dust, and lifteth up the beggar from the dunghill."

And I said to myself, "Oh, God, Oh God! That's me! That's me, apart from Thy wonderful grace." For the only difference between me and that man, I realized, was the grace of God. If I had had no better opportunity and had been born of the same parents, and under the same circumstances as this man, I would have been that man, instead of a sinner saved by grace. And so, before speaking a word to this poor derelict, I cried again, "Oh, God, I thank Thee for Thy wonderful grace." For under similar circumstances of birth, environment and opportunity, I would have been no different, and no better. What a humbling truth grace is! .

What Grace Does

Now we notice what the grace of God does. It not only lifts up the poor and raises up the beggar from the dunghill, and cleans him up and gives him a good meal, and a new suit of clothes, and then says, "Now you're all fixed up. You are on your own now, from here on in. Be careful, and don't go back to the alley again, for if you do, I am not going to help you out again." No, grace doesn't put us on probation. Ah, no! Grace goes deeper than that. It not only lifts *up*, but it lifts *out*. It gives us a new appetite, and a new position, and so Hannah says not only:

> "He raiseth up the poor out of the dust, and lifteth up the beggar from the dunghill"

but she continues:

> "to set them among princes, and to make them inherit the throne of glory" (I Samuel 2:8).

Human words fail completely as we contemplate this: "From the gutter-most to the uttermost." He not only saves, but exalts the poor lost sinner to a place in the first family of heaven. He is adopted as a son in the King's palace, he is made a prince, he is seated in the heavenlies, he is made to sit on the throne, and to reign with Christ. This, beloved, is the grace of God. He not only saves, but he keeps, and so Hannah concludes in verse 9:

> "He will keep the feet of his saints. . .for by strength shall no man prevail" (I Samuel 2:9).

Do you know anything about this grace of God? Ah, the Apostle Peter, he knew, he understood. In the two brief epistles which Peter wrote before he died, he speaks of this grace over and over and over again. It is the theme of his last message to the Church. He opens his first epistle with the words:

> "Grace unto you, and peace, be multiplied" (I Peter 1:2).

And he closes the last epistle with:

> "But grow in grace, and in the knowledge of our Lord and Saviour Jesus Christ" (II Peter 3:18).

Chapter Seventeen

PETER AND THE FOOT-WASHING

Jesus knowing that the Father had given all things into his hands, and that he was come from God, and went to God;
He riseth from supper, and laid aside his garments; and took a towel, and girded himself.
After that he poureth water into a bason, and began to wash the disciples' feet, and to wipe them with the towel wherewith he was girded.

John 13:3-5

THIS strikingly strange account is inserted by John at the close of the passover meal. Jesus had just completed the last meal with His disciples, and now before He leaves with them to the Garden of Gethsemane, He engages in this strange rite of foot-washing. John is the only one of the four gospel writers to record this strange act of our Lord. The other three evangelists are entirely silent in regard to the matter. The foot-washing occurred between the passover feast and the institution of the Lord's supper. Judas was evidently still present, and probably left during the ritual of foot-washing or immediately after, and therefore, we believe was not present at the Lord's supper which followed. This is strongly suggested by verse 2:

"And supper (the passover meal) being ended, the devil having now put into the heart of Judas Iscariot, Simon's son, to betray him;

He riseth from supper" (John 13:2, 4a).

133

Meaning of the Rite

In Palestine and other oriental countries, it was the common practice, when guests came into the house, to be met by servants at the door. At this door stood one or more waterpots of water and convenient basins for the washing of the feet. The servants would remove the open sandals of the guests and wash their feet in preparation for going into the home, and place on them clean sandals in place of those which had been soiled by the way.

This practice was general, and so when Jesus began to wash their feet, this was not a new thing for them at all. The thing which surprised and astonished and confused them was that Jesus, their Master, washed the servants, the disciples' feet instead. This was contrary to all custom. Who in the world had ever heard of a thing like this! And it is, therefore, no wonder Peter said, "Thou shalt never wash my feet." Why, Lord, I ought to wash your feet, instead of you washing mine. It is the business of the servant, not the Master, to wash the feet.

The Great Lesson

Before taking up the tremendously timely and important object lesson which Jesus was trying to teach these disciples, and incidentally us as well, we would like to point out the setting and the circumstances under which our Lord performed this washing of the disciples' feet. I believe it will help us to understand the solemnity of this entire occasion.

The time was just before the agony of Gethsemane and of Calvary. This was the passover evening. In another twelve hours He would be hanging on the Cross. Now Jesus knew all of this beforehand. Notice how the passage is introduced:

"Now before the feast of the passover, when Jesus knew that his hour was come that he should depart out of this world unto the Father, having loved his own which were in the world, he loved them unto the end" (John 13:1).

Notice carefully the expression, "When Jesus *knew* that his hour was come." We must stop for a moment right here. The One who a moment later knelt at the disciples' feet to do the service of a slave, was the Omniscient, Omnipotent, Eternal Son of the living God, the Eternal Creator. "Jesus knew that his hour was come." He knew what lay ahead, every detail of all that lay in the future. Yet this omniscient, all-knowing, all-wise, all-powerful Creator was now about to stoop to washing His creatures' feet!

One would imagine that Jesus in this hour would be occupied with other thoughts than His disciples' soiled feet. With the agony of the Garden and the Cross only a few hours away, one would imagine that He would be occupied with the horror of that which lay before Him. One would imagine that He would be occupied in seeking sympathy, or help and service from these disciples, but instead He seems to be utterly oblivious to His own sorrow, to His own need, and is so completely, compellingly overpowered and consumed with love for His disciples who would leave Him in just a few hours, that He forgets all about the Cross, or at least He makes no reference to it whatsoever.

What Hour?

We ask, therefore, the question, What hour did our Lord refer to? We would think it would be that dread hour of suffering and agony that would culminate in the bitter acme of the infinite cry of utter loneliness: "My God, My God, Why hast Thou forsaken Me?" But no! if we read carefully this passage, we find that He was not thinking of this hour. This is not the hour He was referring to, for the passage reads:

"When Jesus knew that his hour was come that he should depart out of this world unto the Father. . ."

We ought to read this carefully. Our Lord and Saviour passes by the Cross entirely, never even mentioning it, but thinks of the need of His disciples after He will leave them, to go again to the Father. What matchless, incomprehensible love is this? With Gethsemane an hour away, and Calvary a few hours later, the Saviour is concerned about His disciples rather than Himself. Concerned, I say, with a dozen men, one who would betray Him, another who would deny Him, another who would doubt Him, and all of whom would forsake Him. For remember, Jesus *knew* all of this.

AMAZING LOVE

It is only with the greatest difficulty that we can even try to express the depth of love in the setting in this wonderful verse. This truly is divine love: this is supernatural love indeed, and so we are not surprised at the way the verse ends:

"Having loved his own which were in the world, he loved them unto the end (unto the uttermost)" (John 13:1).

Deep indeed are the lessons here, important and valuable. The eternal Son of God, the Creator of the universe, knowing how soon these disciples would forsake Him, was nevertheless willing to become their servant. Oh, how we need the lesson of the washing of one another's feet.

How hard it is for us to forgive! How difficult to return good for evil! Yet therein lies the dignity and glory of the inscrutable depth of our Saviour's love, that He could love the unlovely, the unloving and the unlovable. Yes, Jesus knew all about it, but:

"Having loved his own which were in the world, he loved them unto the end" (John 13:1).

THE ETERNAL GOD

We dwell at length on this lesson hidden here, because it is made so emphatic by the Holy Spirit in our Scripture. It is repeated again in verse 3:

"Jesus *knowing* that the Father had given all things into his hands, and that he was come from God, and went to God;

He riseth from supper, and laid aside his garments. . . and began to wash the disciples' feet" (John 13:3-5).

What a portrait of His incarnation! To wash us from our sins (for this rite becomes a parable of instruction), He laid aside His glory and came in the attire of a servant. Notice the detail given by the Holy Spirit. Why does not the record simply state: "And after supper Jesus washed His disciples' feet." That would have been enough to convey to us His condescension. But no, the Spirit gives every little detail of this entire ceremony. Here they are. Note them carefully.

1. Jesus was the all-knowing One.
2. He riseth from supper.
3. He laid aside His garments.
4. He took a towel and tied it about Him.
5. He poured water into a basin.
6. He washed His disciples' feet.
7. He dried them with the towel.

WHY ALL THIS DETAIL?

Again we ask, Why all this detail? Why not the simple statement by itself? There must, of course, be a definite reason, and while we undoubtedly do not see the full meaning of each little detail, we do see very clearly outlined a picture of our Saviour in His coming to earth to cleanse and to purify His Church, the Bride for which He was to lay down His life.

Remember that He was deity. He was God. From a beginningless eternity He had been God, and then for the great love wherewith He loved us, He laid aside that form of God nineteen hundred years ago, and left His high exalted position of Master and Lord of creation. He laid aside His glorious garments and having laid aside His vesture of the form of God, He takes a towel, the badge of the lowliest of servants, and girds Himself with it, then He pours water into a basin and washes the feet of His disciples.

Notice the teaching here. First He laid aside His garments, then He assumed the attire of the servant. Here truly is deity taking on humanity. He left His glory above, laid aside the form of God, took on Him our human nature, born of a woman, a man of flesh and of bone, and then girded Himself with a towel, the symbol of servitude and slavery, when "the Word became flesh."

The water is the cleansing of the Word of God. After Jesus had laid aside His glory, and in the garb of humanity had gone to the Cross, He sends His Holy Spirit to inspire this Book, that by this Word we, though unworthy, might be cleansed and have eternal life. Unfathomable depths of the Love of God! Wonderful grace of our loving Lord!

This and infinitely more, we believe, is the lesson of the washing of the disciples' feet, wholly apart from the physical, literal rite. In the next chapter we shall see the "doctrine" which is contained here, as well as the great practical object lesson which the Lord left for our example.

However, before closing this chapter, we confess that we feel deeply our inability to express more of the infinite depth and unfathomable scope of the love of Christ as expressed in this wonderful, wonderful record. We feel deeply our miserable failure in not being able to put into human words something of the infinite love of our lovely Lord which so often we do feel within our hearts, but find so difficult to express. Truly we can echo the words of that hymn:

> Could we with ink the ocean fill,
> And were the skies of parchment made.
> Were every stalk on earth a quill,
> And every man a scribe by trade.
> To write the love of God above,
> Would drain the ocean dry.
> Nor could the scroll contain the whole,
> Though stretched from sky to sky.

Or with Paul, as we think of the fact that the Lord laid aside His glory, and came to dwell in human flesh, and became a servant, we repeat with him:

"Let this mind be in you, which was also in Christ Jesus:

Who, being in the form of God thought it not robbery to be equal with God:

But made himself of no reputation, and took upon him the form of a servant, and was made in the likeness of men:

And being found in fashion as a man, he humbled himself, and became obedient unto death, even the death of the cross" (Philippians 2:5-8).

Chapter Eighteen

THE BREAD OF LIFE

He riseth from supper, and laid aside his garments; and took a towel, and girded himself.

After that he poured water into a bason, and began to wash the disciples' feet, and to wipe them with the towel wherewith he was girded.

Then cometh he to Simon Peter: and Peter saith unto him, Lord dost thou wash my feet?

Jesus answered and said unto him, What I do thou knowest not now; but thou shalt know hereafter.

Peter saith unto him, Thou shalt never wash my feet.

Jesus answered him, if I wash thee not, thou hast no part with me.

Simon Peter saith unto him, Lord, not my feet only, but also my hands and my head.

John 13:4-9

THERE are few passages in the Scriptures more full of instruction, richer in doctrine, more timely in practical application, than this record of the washing of the disciples' feet by the Lord Jesus. We shall, I am sure, never be able to comprehend fully the final depths of this wonderful teaching. It was far more than just a rite or ordinance to be religiously observed by us. There are those among Christendom who believe and teach that we are to follow the literal example of the Lord Jesus, and practice literal foot-washing of one another's feet, and place it alongside the Lord's Supper and Baptism as an equally important ordinance to be observed.

No Quarrel with Foot-washers

I have absolutely no quarrel with anyone who sincerely believes that foot-washing should be literally practiced by believers today. If you honestly feel that the Lord would have you wash one another's feet, I certainly would raise no objection to it. By all means do what you believe to be the will of the Lord. I will go even farther than this. If I were living in a community where the only place I could find fellowship were in an assembly where foot-washing was practiced, I should, without violating my conscience seek fellowship with them, and if I could have no fellowship unless I observed their foot-washing, I would gladly wash the brethren's feet. I would consider my Christian fellowship too important to spoil it by quibbling or arguing about the meaning of an ordinance which has no saving value at all, and is a matter of personal opinion. Even though I might not believe that it was obligatory to observe this in a literal way, I believe for the sake of fellowship we ought to make some concessions, and if this could be done today, there would be less of reproach upon the testimony of Christ.

The Real Lesson

I want to emphasize one fundamental fact. There is something far more important than practicing literal foot-washing. It is practicing the "spirit" of the act, rather than the act itself. The foot-washing which Jesus performed was a spiritual object lesson, an example of service, humility, and of love. It is far more important to learn the lesson which it teaches, than to observe it merely as an ordinance or a religious practice. This is true of every ordinance in the

Bible. Spiritual ordinances are for spiritual people, and must be spiritually discerned, or they can be of absolutely no value or help to us at all. Unless we recognize the spiritual meaning of any Christian act, our observance becomes merely an empty formalism, a barren, religious act, a mere observance of the letter of the law, while missing the spirit of the act entirely.

An Example

As an example of this we refer you to the words of our Lord Jesus Christ on another occasion, but which I think will illustrate what we mean. In John 6, Jesus in speaking to His disciples says:

> "Verily, verily, I say unto you, Except ye eat the flesh of the Son of man, and drink his blood, ye have no life in you.
>
> For my flesh is meat indeed, and my blood is drink indeed.
>
> He that eateth my flesh, and drinketh my blood, dwelleth in me, and I in him" (John 6:53, 55-56).

Now what did the Lord Jesus Christ mean by this strange statement about eating His flesh and drinking His blood? Did He mean that we were to eat His literal, physical flesh, and drink His literal, physical blood? The disciples evidently thought this was what Jesus meant, and it caused utter confusion among them. How can we eat His flesh and drink His blood? How can we today, nineteen hundred years after, when that body has already gone to heaven, and has been gone almost two millenniums, still eat His body, and drink His blood? No wonder then that the Church has tried in every way to answer this problem, but has never come to full agreement. The Roman Catholic Church seeks to solve it by the teaching of the doctrine of "trans-substantiation."

This Catholic doctrine teaches that the bread or the wafer at the Eucharist, and the wine, is mysteriously and miraculously changed, by the blessing of the priest, into the literal flesh and blood of the Lord Jesus Christ. If we accept this explanation, then, of course, the question is answered as far as we are concerned.

The Lutheran church, however, has met the question in quite another way. They teach the doctrine of "consubstantiation." While rejecting the teaching that the bread and the wine in the Lord's Supper is totally transformed into the flesh of Christ's body, and His blood, they teach that "in and under" the physical elements of bread and wine, the body and blood of the Lord Jesus Christ are somehow mysteriously present. In this way they seek to understand the meaning of the words of our Lord when He said:

"Except ye eat the flesh of the Son of man, and drink his blood, ye have no life in you" (John 6:53).

It is no wonder that the great Reformers, Zwingli and Calvin, broke on this knotty question. Zwingli insisted that the flesh and blood were symbolic, while Calvin insisted that it was the literal body, and blood of the Lord.

THE DISCIPLES' PROBLEM

But let us not be too hasty to condemn those who hold to this literal interpretation, for even the disciples were confused, and in John 6:60 we read this:

"Many therefore of his disciples, when they had heard this, said, This is an hard saying; who can hear it?" (John 6:60).

"From that time many of his disciples went back, and walked no more with him" (John 6:66).

Many disciples broke with our Lord over this particular problem which we are discussing, and called it a "hard saying."

However, if we study the context and Jesus' own interpretation, which He Himself gives, we should be able to arrive at a satisfactory answer. It is always dangerous to take a single passage or a single verse by itself, for doing this leads to all sorts of confusion. We must, in studying the Scriptures, always read it in the light of the setting, and ask yourselves, what is Jesus talking about in this particular chapter? Remember, this is the great discourse on the Bread of Life. He reminds them how their fathers ate manna in the wilderness. and then says:

"I am that bread of life" (John 6:48).

"Your fathers did eat manna in the wilderness, and are dead.

This is the bread which cometh down from heaven, that a man may eat thereof, and not die.

I am the living bread which came down from heaven: if any man eat of this bread, he shall live forever: and the bread that I will give is my flesh, which I will give for the life of the world" (John 6:49-51).

The manna in the wilderness was, therefore, typical of the Body of the Lord Jesus Christ. It pointed to the Cross where He would die, and give His life for our salvation. But the manna which came down from heaven was not His literal Body, but it pointed forward to His sacrifice when He would become our spiritual bread, our source of spiritual life, and our spiritual sustenance, even as the manna was for the children of Israel in the wilderness. And then follows this statement:

"Whoso eateth my flesh, and drinketh my blood, hath eternal life" (John 6:54).

This spiritual significance was missed by the disciples entirely, and they thought only of His physical flesh and His material blood, and they shrank from the gruesome thought, and many of them walked no more with Him. It is then that Jesus gives His interpretation to those who remained behind. He explains and clears up the entire subject. Follow carefully the words of our Lord:

"When Jesus knew in himself that his disciples murmured at it, he said unto them, Doth this offend you?

What and if ye shall see the Son of man ascend up where he was before?" (John 6:61-62)

Now here we have the key to the entire problem. He seems to say, you have difficulty understanding how you can eat my flesh *now* while I am here, but what about it when I am gone and my Body is not here any more? When I have ascended up to My Father? That will be an even greater problem than doing it now, while I am still bodily present.

THE ANSWER

And then it is that Jesus explains it all in the next verse. He says in essence, I am not speaking about my literal flesh and blood at all, but the spiritual. Notice, therefore, our Lord's answer:

"It is the spirit that quickeneth; the flesh profiteth nothing: the *words* that I speak unto you, they are spirit, and they are life" (John 6:63).

In this passage we are to note carefully three things in this respect:

1. It is the Spirit that makes alive.
2. The flesh profiteth *nothing*.
3. The words that I speak unto you, they are spirit, and they are life.

It is, therefore, the Spirit of the act—the flesh profiteth nothing. Even if you could literally eat My flesh, says the Lord, it would not benefit you at all, if you do not understand the spiritual meaning, and the lesson I am seeking to teach. And the lesson He is teaching is simply this: "We are to feed on Him, not by eating His body, or drinking His blood, but by receiving His Word, feasting on the spiritual food of the Word of God, concerning His sacrifice for us. To observe only the letter of the law is to remain forever in death.

THE LORD'S SUPPER

The same is true of the Lord's Supper. Eating a piece of bread or a wafer and sipping a swallow of wine or juice, is an utterly empty, meaningless, religious ritual, *unless* we understand what it spiritually represents.

While physical elements are used in the Lord's Supper, such as the bread and the cup, or as some use it, wine, the elements themselves are not the important thing, but the Spirit and the lesson which they teach. There are those who believe in using unleavened bread; others use leavened bread. Some insist upon using fermented wine, while others insist upon using only the unfermented juice of the grape. If the devil can keep us busy arguing about these material details, and miss the spirit of the ordinance, he has accomplished exactly what he set out to do. These elements are merely used to point us to something higher.

As we take the bread, it acts only as a reminder of how His Body was broken for us, and we are lost in the contemplation of His wonderful sacrifice in our behalf, and forget all about the material element which was only an introduction to our spiritual experience. We are not concerned at all as to the way in which it is broken or the way in which it is served, or what kind of bread it is. The same is true of the cup. When we lift it to our lips, we are lost in contemplation, and lifted above the material of the ordinance and the physical elements until we are lost in our contemplation of His wonderful love, and the shedding of His precious blood, so that the physical elements which are being used are lost sight of entirely, and disappear in the background.

We are to fix our minds on the spiritual bread, and forget the material; and think of His blood and not the physical element in the cup. Let us remember, Jesus said, "it is the spirit that quickeneth; the flesh profiteth nothing." The very same thing is true of baptism. Unless we understand its spiritual significance and meaning, and what it represents, the ordinance itself can be of absolutely no help to us. What we say concerning this applies also to the rite of foot-washing. The literal, physical foot-washing is entirely secondary, whether it is practiced or whether it is not, with warm water or cold, as long as we understand, accept and profit by the lesson which the Lord Jesus is seeking to teach us. We become so occupied with the mechanics of these things, and the little details which are wholly insignificant, that we lose the spiritual meaning entirely. This then we believe to be the teaching of the Lord Jesus Christ when He says to His disciples in verse 12:

"Know ye what I have done to you?

Ye call me Master and Lord: and ye say well; for so I am.

If I then, your Lord and Master, have washed your feet; ye also ought to wash one another's feet.

For I have given you an example, that ye should do as I have done to you" (John 13:12-15).

The entire exercise was an object lesson, an example which He set before us, so that we might be satisfied, not merely with the literal act of foot-washing, but might practice the spirit of the act, the spirit of humility and service, and willingness to take the place of the lowliest servant.

Chapter Nineteen

REGENERATION AND RESTORATION

Simon Peter saith unto him, Lord, not my feet only, but also my hands and my head.
Jesus saith to him, He that is washed needeth not save to wash his feet, but is clean every whit.

John 13:9-10

IMPETUOUS, blustering, blundering, spouting Simon Peter! What an unpredictable disciple he was, and yet withal, we cannot help but love him at least for his frankness and bluntness, for one always knew where Simon Peter stood. Our Lord also knew that He could use the life and the actions and the conduct of Peter to bring out some tremendous truths which might have otherwise been lost to us. Jesus, on the very eve of His death, was teaching His disciples a much-needed lesson in humility, forgiveness, patience, love and service, which few of us have learned as we should, and He illustrates this by a dramatic ritual, the washing of His disciple's feet.

We have already seen the practical lesson of humility and service which our Lord taught in this act. But there is far more than practical instruction and exhortation to love and forbear one another. There is far more than merely a picture of the Lord Jesus laying aside His glory and taking on Him the form of a man to save us from our sins. All this is truly precious, and therefore, we have given it precedence. But in this passage the Lord also declares a tremendous

148

and important doctrine, the doctrine of the grace of God. It is the doctrine of the security of the believer, and Simon Peter is to be the subject through whom our Lord is to bring out this great and wonderful and much-misunderstood truth.

PETER'S OBJECTION

After Jesus had girded Himself with a towel (symbol of servitude) He began to wash His disciples' feet. Which disciple was first we are not told, and it would be needless to speculate. There is every reason to believe that Judas Iscariot himself was present at this foot-washing, and beheld the action of his Master whom he was so soon to betray. However, we do not believe that the Lord washed Judas' feet, but that for some reason or another he must have been skipped, as we shall see from the lesson which our Lord is seeking to teach in this particular instance. It seems that Peter was one of the last ones on the list, for we are told that when He came to Peter, he raised a serious objection. Peter evidently had been watching with a great deal of amazement and wonder as Jesus went from one disciple to the other. He simply could not understand the meaning of all this, and so when Jesus comes finally to Simon Peter, he vehemently objects and he blurts out:

"Dost thou wash *my* feet?"

This was more than a question on the part of Peter. It was a firm declaration of refusal. You, *You*, my Lord and my Master, You wash my feet? Why, Lord, I should wash your feet!

Then Jesus says to him, Peter you just don't understand. My feet do not happen to be soiled like yours, for I am the holy one of God, I am not defiled by the world, as you have been. I am perfectly clean and free from all sin and defilement, and therefore, am the proper One to wash your feet.

But Peter, with you it is quite different. Your feet do need washing, and you shall soon find out how badly you need it. You have been defiled,

> "What I do thou knowest not now; but thou shalt know hereafter" (John 13:7).

Notice the expression, "thou shalt know hereafter." How soon thereafter Peter was to find out, and learn this great need of continual cleansing, for within a few hours this man who said,"I will die for Thee," and who said, "Dost thou wash my feet?" would whimper and cower before an accusing maid, in the high priest's hall, and curse and swear that he did not even know Christ. Our Saviour's words, therefore, "thou shalt know hereafter (and very soon)" were somewhat prophetic of Peter's denial and his need for forgiveness and for cleansing.

Still Peter did not understand, however. He was so cock-sure of himself that he makes it even more emphatic and says:

> "Thou shalt never wash my feet" (John 13:8).

Poor, poor Simon Peter. How little he knew his own heart! In his devotion for his Lord, which no one can question, he felt he never would fall, he never could be untrue to his Saviour, he would never again be defiled, and, therefore, would never need cleansing again. He did not need any cleansing, ever again. But Jesus knew better. He knew how soon Simon Peter would fail and fall, and so He disillusions him in a moment, and He says:

> "If I wash thee not, thou hast no part with me" (John 13:8).

That was entirely too much for poor Peter. Of course, he did not yet understand the importance of this rite, but if it **was so** important, that he could have no part with the Lord unless He should wash his feet, then why stop with the feet only? Why not give him a complete bath, hands and head and all the members? And then follows the profound teaching of our precious Lord, that one only needs the washing of the body once, but many, many cleansings of the feet. Here is the way the Lord put it:

"He that is washed needeth not save to wash his feet, but is clean every whit" (John 13:10).

Now the underlying figure here is of an oriental returning from his bath house, either public or private. These bath houses were usually in a building apart from the rest of the dwelling. After the bathing had been completed, the person would walk to his home, but on the way to his home he would again soil his feet, wearing the open sandals customarily worn in those days. Upon arriving at his house, therefore, he would be met at the door by the servants who removed his sandals, washed his soiled feet in a basin, and then placed on him clean sandals, before he went into the house.

WASHING OF REGENERATION

So too the believer, when he receives Christ, is bathed and washed clean by the Word of God, and by the blood of Christ. This happens once for all, and is never, never, according to our Lord Jesus, to be repeated. He is saved and justified and forever secure in Him. But while he journeys through this world he still becomes defiled in his walk, conduct and contact with the world round about him, and needs to be cleansed from his defilement over and over again. The blood of the Lord Jesus once applied by faith, answers forever the demands of God's holiness, and forever removes the guilt and the condemnation of sin. It is a picture of the new birth occurring once and for all at the beginning of our Christian life and experience. That bath of regeneration settles the believer's position forever, but in spite of this he needs a provision for constant cleansing from the sins of the flesh which constantly beset him and cling to him because of the presence of the old nature, and because of our sojourn in this world. In Titus 3:5 we read:

> "According to his mercy he saved us, by the washing of regeneration."

Literally it is the "bathing" or "the bath" of regeneration. Jesus said we "must be born again by the water and by the Spirit" (John 3:5). This is the new birth—born from above, not born again and again and again. But while the believer is safe *in Christ,* he is still weak and faulty and sinful in himself.

PETER'S LESSON

This was the lesson Jesus sought to teach Peter and the disciples, and which we also need to learn. By demanding a "second" bathing, Peter was denying the doctrine of salvation by grace. He seems to say, "I have been bathed once, Lord, but I've lost it all again, and need to be bathed all over again. I was saved once, but I have lost my salvation, so — not my feet only, but also my head and my hands, and my entire body."

Jesus soon dispels Peter's fears, however, and says, No, Peter, No. One washing of regeneration, once for all, is sufficient. All you need now is cleansing. And He adds:

> "He that is washed needed not save to wash his feet, but is clean every whit" (John 13:10).

Salvation is the work of God, and God alone, and since it is the work of God, it must be a perfect, faultless work, and, therefore, it can never fail. But man, even after he is saved, does fail, and for this he needs to be cleansed by confession, by repentance, by faith in Christ's forgiveness. How significant, therefore, that Christ should address this to Peter, for in just

a few hours from now, Peter the disciple, would disown his
Lord, curse and swear and lie and forsake Him.

The Lord knew how Peter would fail before He even
saved him, and He made provision even for Peter's failings.
There was cleansing and forgiveness for poor Simon Peter.
And this great lesson of the foot-washing was no doubt Jesus'
way of preparing Peter for his terrible experience. Undoubtedly Simon Peter after he realized what he had done, and had
gone out to weep bitterly outside the court of the high priest's
palace, must have imagined that he was lost again, or had
never even been saved. He might have given up in despair
completely. And then he remembered the words of the Lord
Jesus when He said:

> "He that is washed needeth not save to wash his feet,
> but is clean every whit."

This is the thing that must have given Peter courage, and he
came back again to his Lord, later on.

ETERNAL LIFE

Eternal life, then, is not only eternal, but it is also everlasting. Do you realize that when Jesus washed Peter's feet, He
knew what Peter would do before the morning should dawn?
Yet knowing how terrible Peter would sin, He nevertheless
washes his feet.

Since the Lord knows all things, He must also of necessity
know beforehand all the failures of all God's people whom He
saves. Yes, our God knows, and has made provision for our
cleansing, for our forgiveness, for our restoration, and for our
renewal of joy and power. How significant, therefore, the
words in verse 1:

> "Having loved his own which were in the world, he
> loved them unto the uttermost" (John 13:1).

If We Confess

Before we close this particular chapter I want to press this home to those of you who are conscious of your own weakness, and your own defilement. If you are not conscious that you are still imperfect and constantly defiled by the things of this world, these words will mean little to you until you learn the lesson which Jesus teaches in this foot-washing.

You have received Christ and trusted Him, but like Peter, you, too, have such a struggle. If that is your confession, then listen carefully. It is such a battle, is it not, to go through this life surrounded by all the evil which constantly besets us? You fail and you stumble and you fall until sometimes you wonder whether you are saved at all. You are beset by doubts and fears, your old nature keeps coming up and prodding you again and again. You have to confess over and over, "I know that in me, that is in my flesh, there dwelleth no good thing." You too have cried out, "O wretched man that I am. Who shall deliver me from the body of this death?"

Listen, then, my friend, Jesus has wonderful news for you.

To those of you who are not conscious of any struggle, however, who claim to have no sin or weakness, we only pray that God may awaken you to a realization of your own utter unworthiness. But if you do confess that you are having a battle, then Jesus says, there is forgiveness, and cleansing, and renewal and power. The very consciousness of your failure, the very battle within you is the sign of life. Lack of a sense of sin, absence of a realization of our own wicked heart and failures, can only be the peace of death. True holiness results in a consciousness of our own unworthiness, and sinfulness.

Oh, I realize that Satan would tell us that we are lost again, just to keep us from coming to Christ for the washing of our feet, but such is not the case. John tells us definitely in I John 1:8,

> "If we say that we have no sin, we deceive ourselves, and the truth is not in us."

Again he says in verse 10:

> "If we say that we have not sinned, we make him a liar, and his word is not in us."

These are serious charges, and it will do us no good to deny the facts of life. But now inserted between these two verses John has placed verse 9:

> "If we confess our sins, he is faithful and just to forgive us our sins, and to cleanse us from all unrighteousness."

Our only hope lies, not in denying or closing our eyes to realities, but in honestly and sincerely facing our own unworthiness, and then casting ourselves anew and afresh upon the perfection, upon the holiness, upon the forgiveness and compassion of our loving Saviour, who before we were saved, realized how far short we would come.

No matter what your struggle may be, no matter what your besetting sin may be, no matter how often you may have failed, like Peter you can come to Him, not only to receive forgiveness, but also like Peter to receive new power to conquer that thing, and to live the life of victory day by day.

Chapter Twenty

THREE MISSING THINGS

Jesus saith to him, He that is washed needeth not save to wash his feet, but is clean every whit.

John 13:10

THIS was the answer of our Lord to Simon Peter when he impetuously refused to allow his Saviour to wash his feet, but insisted that also his hands and his head be washed as well. Our Lord reminds Peter that he has already been washed once, and is perfectly clean, and needs only to have his feet cleansed from the defilement of the world and of the flesh. It is a picture of the believer washed in the blood of the Lord Jesus once for all, justified, and complete in Him, and never to be repeated. This is the washing of regeneration. Paul says in Titus:

> "Not by works of righteousness which we have done, but according to his mercy he saved us, by the washing (bathing) of regeneration, and renewing of the Holy Ghost" (Titus 3:5).

This settles forever the believer's position and standing in the Lord Jesus Christ. It establishes his relationship to Christ Jesus forever. This is the washing of regeneration to which Jesus refers when He says:

> "He that is washed. . .is clean every whit."

Daily Defilement

Paul asserts in I Corinthians 6, and verse 11, the following:
"And such were some of you; but ye are *washed*, but

156

ye are sanctified, but ye are justified in the name of the
Lord Jesus, and by the Spirit of our God."

The believer according to Paul, then, is washed in the
blood of the Lord Jesus by the water of the word, sanctified
by the Spirit of God, justified by his faith in Christ. God,
when He now looks upon the believer beholds him as being
perfect in Christ. God looks at every believer *in* Christ, and
reckons the righteousness of Christ to *his* account. *But* this
"washed" believer, this sanctified, separated saint, this justified
child of God, complete in Him, is still in this world and in
contact with its defilement, and subject to the weakness and
the presence of the old nature within him, and in constant
danger of being defiled, and, therefore, stands in daily need
of cleansing from the defilement of sin.

Our Lord Jesus knew before He ever saved us what
miserable failures we would be *after* we were saved. This is
a truth which needs repeating. He knew before He saved
Peter, how he would blunder and fail and stumble, and so
instead of casting him off when he fell, He made provision
for his restoration and his cleansing. This is a truth overlooked
by too many believers, causing untold confusion.

At this point we remind you again of John's words:

"If we confess our sins, he is faithful and just to forgive us our sins, and to cleanse us from all unrighteousness" (I John 1:9).

We repeat, this is for believers. John says, "If *we* confess."
He includes himself in this group. We ought not to sin, to
be sure; we are never excusable when we do, and will have to
pay the penalty, but the fact remains that it is quite impossible
to live in this wicked world without coming in contact with
its defilement constantly, and therefore we need repeated

cleansing. How wonderfully He has made this provision for us! In I John 2:1, we read:

"My little children, these things write I unto you, that ye sin not. And if any man sin, we have an advocate with the Father, Jesus Christ the righteous."

The believer should not sin, there is never an excuse for it, but when he does, and God knows how prone we are to fail, he has also made a provision, for He knew beforehand how prone the old nature is to sin. And so He stands ever ready to cleanse and to wash our feet.

New Testament Priests

The believer is a priest, and the priest must be clean. "They that bear the vessels of the Lord must be clean." This was already foreshadowed in the Old Testament ritual of the service of the priests in the tabernacle and the temple. In Israel the tabernacle of the congregation was the one peculiar place of service for the priesthood. This tabernacle was divided into three parts—the court of the Gentiles, the Holy Place, and then the Holy of Holies. In the outer court stood the altar of burnt offering, and the brazen laver. In the Holy Place stood the table of shewbread, the golden candlestick, and the golden altar of incense. And then in the Holy of Holies, behind the veil, stood the ark of the covenant and the mercy seat.

There were three things missing in this tabernacle, however, which one would expect to find in any well-ordered place of worship, or home. These three missing things were:

1. Windows
2. Chairs
3. A floor

There were no windows in the tabernacle. The only light

came from the seven-branched golden candlestick. The priests were to serve only by the light of this lamp, the Word of God fed by the oil of the Spirit of God. The priest was never to walk by the outside light of nature which would come through artificial windows, but only by the light of the Word illumined by the Holy Spirit.

The second missing thing was a chair. The Old Testament priest could never sit down. His work was never, never done. The people whom the priest represented needed constant help and cleansing every day and hour, and so their work was never completely done. That, of course, was the Old Testament priesthood which was only typical. However, when the Lord Jesus Christ, our great High Priest came, He finished the work and "sat down." In Hebrews 10:11 we read of this:

"And every priest *standeth* daily ministering and offering oftentimes the same sacrifices, which can never take away sins:

But this man, after he had offered one sacrifice for sins for ever, *sat down* on the right hand of God;

For by one offering he hath perfected for ever them that are sanctified" (Hebrews 10:11-12, 14).

The work, therefore, is done and all who believe on Jesus Christ are sanctified and perfected in Him forever. But these, who are sanctified and perfect *in Christ* are still in the world and subject to its defilement. And that brings us to the third "missing thing" in this tabernacle of the congregation.

The tabernacle had no floor except the ground upon which the priest walked all day long. Whenever the tabernacle was set up, it was placed right upon the ground. The priest, therefore, in his ministry of the holy service of God was constantly in contact with the earth. His feet were soiled each step he took, by the very ground on which he was compelled to walk even while serving God. But the priest must be clean. And so a provision for repeated washing of these feet must be provided, and this we find in the court of the tabernacle. At the very entrance of the holy place stood a brazen laver or basin with water for this very purpose, and every time the priest entered the holy place to serve, he must stop at the laver to wash his feet.

Not Whole Body

"And the Lord spake unto Moses, saying,

Thou shalt also make a laver of brass, and his foot also of brass, to wash withal: and thou shalt put it between the tabernacle of the congregation and the altar, and thou shalt put water therein.

For Aaron and his sons shall wash their hands and their feet thereat" (Exodus 30:17-19).

Notice where this basin for the foot-washing of the priests was commanded to be placed. It was between the tabernacle and the altar. The altar was the place of sacrifice; the tabernacle was the place of service, fellowship and worship. At the altar (type of the Cross) complete salvation was provided, but before the priest, who already had been to the altar for justification and salvation, could enter into communion and fellowship, he constantly had to have his feet washed. The order is first the Altar, the Cross; then the laver of cleansing. At the altar the guilt of sin is taken care of; at the laver cleansing for fellowship is provided.

Bathing and Washing

We must remember, however, that this washing of the feet was not the first bathing the priests underwent. In the consecration of the priesthood the order was the same as that which Christ laid down in the thirteenth chapter of

John. First, the complete bath, and then the repeated foot-washings. This order was also followed in the consecration of the priest. At the beginning of a priest's ministry, he was given a complete washing in water. This was once for all, at the outset of his consecration. This ceremonial bathing occurred only once. In Exodus 29:4 we read:

"And Aaron and his sons thou shalt bring unto the door of the tabernacle of the congregation, and shalt wash them with water."

This was the inaugural washing to which Jesus evidently referred when He said to Peter:

"He that is washed needeth not save to wash his feet, but is clean every whit" (John 13:10).

This is again restated in Leviticus 8 and verse 6:

"And Moses brought Aaron and his sons, and washed them with water."

This was at the beginning of their induction into the priest-hood. After this came the laver. At the altar the priest had been washed once for all. But after the priest had been washed and justified at the altar, next follows his sanctification for service, worship and communion. Every time he approached the tabernacle he must stop at the laver. The record is found in Exodus 30:18:

"Thou shalt also make a laver of brass. . .and thou shalt put water therein.

For Aaron and his sons shall wash their hands and their feet thereat:

When they go into the tabernacle of the congregation, they shall wash with water, that they die not; or when they come near to the altar to minister, to burn offering made by fire unto the Lord:

So they shall wash their hands and their feet, that

they die not: and it shall be a statute for ever" (Exodus 30:18-21).

This is the sanctification and cleansing taught by Jesus in the washing of the disciples' feet.

Not a Single Act

This cleansing and sanctification was not a single act, but was to be repeated as often as necessary. It was a daily experience for the priest in the tabernacle. While the fire upon the altar never went out, and the ceremonial washing of consecration was never repeated, the washing of the feet of the Priests must be repeated. It must be done every time the priest's feet approached the altar of the tabernacle, for his feet were constantly defiled by his contact with the earth upon which he walked. This is because there was *no* floor in the tabernacle, and so provision must be made for the repeated washing of the feet, so graphically portrayed by our Lord in John 13. How often Peter must have remembered it, and how happy he must have been for its provision. In the days ahead when Peter denied his Lord, when he became discouraged and went back to fishing, when he acted in haste after Pentecost, how his mind must have gone back to Jesus' words:

"What I do thou knowest not now; but thou shalt know hereafter" (John 13:7).

Oh, how we do rejoice in the provision for cleansing! What day is there when at evening we can look back without having to say, "Lord, I have again come short. I have not been all that I should have been. I have neglected to do some things that I might have done, and I have done some things I fear will not meet with Thy approval." What a sweet sense of comfort and peace and rest it then brings to our heart to remember our precious Lord's teaching in this rite.

Chapter Twenty-one

SIMON PETER'S BROTHER

One of the two which heard John speak, and followed him, was Andrew, Simon Peter's brother.
He first findeth his own brother Simon, and saith unto him, We have found the Messias, which is being interpreted, the Christ.
And he brought him to Jesus.

John 1:40-42

ANDREW, Simon Peter's brother, has been so completely overshadowed by his famous brother, Simon Peter, that he has been almost lost in obscurity. And yet without Andrew there would not have been a Peter, for it was poor, neglected, obscure Andrew who introduced Simon to Jesus, and he in turn became Peter. In these chapters on Peter, we, therefore, want to devote some discussion to his obscure but wonderful brother, Andrew.

Andrew never preached a sermon, he never wrote a book, he held no special office; and he is mentioned only a few times in the entire record of the gospels. He was evidently not endowed with any great gift of personality.

Andrew is mentioned just thirteen times in the gospels; twice by Matthew, four times by Mark, twice by Luke. He is mentioned only once in the book of the Acts. However, it is John who uses his name five times and tells us about all we know about this obscure, but truly remarkable

163

disciple of Christ. For while Andrew never preached a sermon, he never denied his Lord either. While he never wrote a book, he never cursed and swore that he did not know the Lord either.

John, we said, tells us all that we know about this interesting character. The other writers mention him only in connection with the other disciples. But in the three incidents which John records for us, we get a world of information about this colorless, yet remarkable man. Even his name is a plain name, as plain as a name can be. The name, Andrew, comes from the word, "Aner," and means "a man." He was just an ordinary man. There was nothing outstanding or remarkable about him which attracted the attention of others. He lived his life in a quiet, unpretentious way, yet his ministry was more important, and greater and more far-reaching than that of his Pentecostal preacher brother, Peter. The world saw Peter, but I am sure that God saw Andrew.

THREE INSTANCES

John gives us three pictures of Andrew, all of them similar, and yet quite different. The earliest mention we have of Andrew is in John 1. After finding the Lord Jesus, Andrew immediately sought and found his brother, Simon, and brought him to Jesus. In John 6 Andrew finds a little lad with five cookies and a few sardines with which Jesus fed a multitude of five thousand. Then in John 12 Andrew brings the Greeks to the Lord who had expressed the desire, "We would see Jesus."

That is about all that we know about Andrew. But what volumes these three incidents speak! Andrew, the forgotten, the neglected, the obscure disciple, stands out like a tower of strength among all the apostles, as the man who knew how to bring people to Christ.

Andrew was the personal worker among the disciples, and therefore, largely forgotten. His name did not appear in the papers; his picture never was put in the ads. No, Andrew had no color. He had no background to exploit. He could not entice the crowds by giving his testimony of how God saved him from a life of sin and dope and gambling and drunkenness and prison life. No, Andrew was just a little fellow, known only as the brother of the great preacher, Peter.

Andrew could not report the greatest crowds. All Andrew did was to bring a lad to the Lord Jesus Christ, who became the means of feeding five thousand others. No, Andrew did not amount to a great deal, and while others were basking in the sunlight of popular acclaim, he was leading a crude, ignorant fisherman by the name of Simon to the Lord Jesus, who later was to become the preacher who saw three thousand converted to Christ in one single day.

No, Andrew did not rate high, but he led some Greeks to the Lord Jesus, one of whom tradition tells us was a doctor by the name of Luke, who later was to become the personal companion of the world's greatest preacher, Paul; Dr. Luke who wrote two of the most important books of the New Testament, the gospel that bears his name, and the book of the Acts.

HEAVEN'S SURPRISE

Heaven will be a place of many surprises, I am sure, and one will be to find out the full and complete story of Andrew, who was known for just one thing—he knew how to bring people to Christ, one by one. There will be no "big shots" in heaven. When the books are opened up there, we shall find many, many whom the world never recognized, shining in the glory of their great reward, while many who here rode the crest of popularity, and basked in the limelight, and never knew real sacrifice or want, will have to take a lower seat. "For the first shall be the last, and the last shall be first."

Andrew had but one talent, but he used it to the full. There are others who have ten talents, but will fall short of Andrew's reward, for it is not the bulk, the mass, the visible, but the faithfulness with which we have used what we have which will count in that great day.

The Little Fellow

I am deeply concerned about the little Andrews in the world today. All over this land and throughout the world are men and women, laboring and struggling on meager means, and with few talents, in the out of the way places, finding a lad here, a Simon there, and once in a while a Luke. They go on, unnoticed and unsung, but what a revelation it will be when the Lord of the Harvest reveals what has been accomplished by these little Andrews.

Humanly speaking, without Andrew there would have been no Peter, no preacher for Pentecost; without Andrew no lad with cookies and sardines, and the miracle of five thousand fed; without Andrew, no Doctor Luke to write the gospel. Thank God for the Andrews in our midst, the humble souls who seek no honor from men, no recognition here below, but day by day go about winning men and women, boys and girls for Jesus, and telling them the only story they know, "I have found the Christ. Let me bring you to Him."

Andrew's Reward

What a reward Andrew received! How his heart must have rejoiced to see Jesus feeding that five thousand, to hear Peter preach on Pentecost, and to read (as I hope he lived to do) that scholarly gospel of Luke and the book of Acts. But there is another day coming, when the Lord will fully reward Andrew according to his works. That will be the time when all the other little Andrews are going to come into their own.

ANDREW THE SOWER

Andrew was one of God's sowers. He never reaped a big harvest himself, apparently, but was content to have others reap what he had sown. He sowed a Simon, and Peter reaped a Pentecost. He sowed a little lad, but five thousand were fed. God sees the sowers, however, while men follow the reapers. We love the crowds; Andrew loved individuals. He was content to sow alone, unpraised and unnoticed. David says in Psalm 126:6,

"He that goeth forth and weepeth, bearing precious seed, shall doubtless come again with rejoicing, bringing his sheaves with him."

Sowing is lonely, hard and difficult work, and it is the work of Andrew. It is usually done in the spring when it is raw and cold and wet. It means plowing and toiling. In contrast, reaping is joyous work. It occurs in the beauty of the fall. Sowers work alone. Reapers are always found in crowds. You have never yet seen a picture of "The Sower" with more than one sower in it. It is lonely work to cast the seed and not see the fruit. But in all harvest pictures we see the crowds assembling together in all their gaiety and joy.

When Jesus comes, you forgotten souls who have only had the task of sowing are going to have your day. You faithful ones who pray and weep and testify, you faithful ones in the hard, out of the way places, in that little field, discouraged because you see so little result, your reward is sure. Take heart, for there is a day of reckoning coming, for the Lord has said:

"They that sow in tears shall reap in joy" (Psalm 126:5).

Let me close this chapter with an illustration. Two men go to a gospel meeting. Both of them hear the call to service. Both of them are saved. One dedicates his life to the work of Christ, and the other does not heed the call. Now remember, both of these men are saved, justified, because they have come to Christ, but they have acted differently afterward, and here their ways must part.

The first one goes on to Bible School, then to the Mission field in the heart of Africa. He lives in poverty and want, trying to win men for Christ. He slaves and labors from morn till night, praying, calling, pleading, preaching, kneeling in the dust and dirt, to help poor men and women to know the love of Christ. In a few years his health fails from overwork and fatigue in his zeal to win others to Christ. And then he dies in poverty at an early age, and is buried in a jungle grave.

The other man stays at home. He too is saved, but becomes a successful, Christian business man. He makes a fortune by God's blessing, lives in a mansion, has cars and yachts and servants, receives the best in medical care, eats the proper food, looks after his health, has his check-up with the doctor every six months, lives in luxury to a ripe old age. He endows a college, and has the dormitory named for him, he is generous with his money, for he has plenty of it. He supports missions liberally also, and he is honored by all for his philanthrophy. He is elected to the highest place of honor in the church for his liberality.

But wait a moment! There is a day of reckoning coming, too. The poor missionary has not been forgotten. No one but God knows the pain and the suffering and the sacrifice he endured. Everyone remembers the other man, for his name is emblazoned upon the records for his liberality, for his Christian service, for his money, only a comparatively small portion of which he ever dedicated to the Lord. God remembers all, however, and God knows all the facts.

There will be a time when there will be rewards for the "little Andrews" on the basis of these things. Will both be rewarded alike, or will these inequalities be made right when Jesus comes? The one gave his all, and the other gave much, and yet nothing, for it meant no sacrifice. That, I am sure, is the revelation that will be made at the judgment seat of Christ. You who suffer alone, and forsaken, and unrecognized, take heart, for it was Paul who said in I Corinthians 4:5,

> "Therefore judge nothing before the time, until the Lord come, who both will bring to light the hidden things of darkness, and will make manifest the counsels of the hearts: and then shall every man have praise of God."

Chapter Twenty-two

THE FORGOTTEN PREACHERS

When Jesus then lifted up his eyes, and saw a great company come unto him, he saith unto Philip, Whence shall we buy bread, that these may eat?

Philip answered him, Two hundred pennyworth of bread is not sufficient for them, that every one of them may take a little.

One of his disciples, Andrew, Simon Peter's brother, saith unto him,

There is a lad here, which hath five barley loaves, and two small fishes: but what are they among so many?

And Jesus took the loaves; and when he had given thanks, he distributed to the disciples, and the disciples to them that were set down; and likewise of the fishes as much as they would.

John 6:5, 7-9, 11

THIS is one of the three instances where Andrew, Simon Peter's brother, brought someone to the Lord Jesus Christ. We have already seen in John 1 how he brought his own brother, Simon. Here in John 6 he brings a lad, and finally in John 12 he brings the Greeks who had come up to worship at the feast. These three brief references sum up the entire record of this remarkable personal worker and soul-winner, so often forgotten — Andrew, Simon Peter's brother.

Just in passing we would like to call your attention to the

order in which these three instances occur, as illustrating the great commission of our Lord Jesus Christ. You will recall that Jesus had commanded His disciples:

"That repentance and remission of sin should be preached in his name among all nations, beginning at Jerusalem" (Luke 24:47).

In Acts 1:8 Jesus gives the rest of the order:

"And ye shall be witnesses unto me both in Jerusalem, and in all Judaea, and in Samaria, and unto the uttermost part of the earth" (Acts 1:8).

That was the order in the book of Acts. It is significant that this order is also followed in these three narratives concerning Andrew, the soul winner, who brought Simon, the lad and the Greeks to Christ. I do not suppose that Andrew knew anything about this, but the Holy Spirit evidently had this in mind when He recorded these three instances in the following order:

1. Simon was brought to Christ in Judaea.
2. The little lad was brought to Christ in Samaria.
3. The Greeks whom Andrew led to Christ were from the Gentiles in the far off land of Greece.

We mention this merely in passing, and to remind you that this is the order we are to follow in our soul-winning business as well, beginning at home, and then reaching out from the home base.

First Findeth Simon

After Andrew had found Christ, his first concern was his *own* brother. The record is emphatic:

"He first findeth his *own brother*, Simon" (John 1:41).

What a tremendous lesson this brief verse contains. Andrew began at home. He started at the right place. He recognized

that our first responsibility in winning souls to Christ is right
in our own home. If we cannot win our own loved ones to
Christ, how in the world do we expect to win others to
Him? To go out preaching and singing the Gospel around
the world (no matter how important) cannot meet with
God's approval until we have followed His divine order. I am
sure that if we have not tried our best to win our own loved
ones for Christ first, that these other things cannot be expected
to be blessed of the Lord.

I have known converts, who the day after they were saved,
told me they felt called to go into the ministry, or felt called
to go to Africa or South America, or some other mission field.
Invariably I have asked them, "Have you any unsaved ones
at home, among your family, and your relatives that ought
to be saved first?" And when they admitted they had, I asked,
"Have you tried earnestly to bring them to Christ?"

Better begin with your own brother. Better begin at Jerusalem. You need to practice on your own loved ones first,
before you think beyond the city of Jerusalem.

Most Difficult Place

Of course, I realize that it is the hardest place to begin. It
is far easier to witness to others than to your own family. It
must have been so for Andrew also, for he certainly picked a
most unlikely, unpromising prospect. Simon, the blunderer,
Simon with his loose tongue, his hot temper, his changeable
disposition. Cursing, swearing Simon! He surely could have
picked a bit more likely prospect. But no, we read: "He
first findeth his own brother Simon . . . and he brought him
to Jesus."

I have a Negro preacher friend, a dear brother, who once
gave the answer to this question in a striking way. A group
of students at a Bible and Missionary Institute came to him,

and said: "Brother So-and-So, you will be greatly pleased to
know that we are planning to go as missionaries to Africa
in a few months when we complete our training here, and
bring the gospel to your people there."

They imagined, of course, that he would be elated, and
they were sadly taken aback when he asked them: "How many
of my Negro people have you tried to win for Christ here at
home? You have gone to school three years and lived a
stone's throw from one of the densest Negro populations in the
city. What an opportunity to reach my people right here
at home! How many of these have you won for Christ?"

It was a good question, and I cannot blame him for his
blunt rejoinder, for I know what a burden this brother has
for his colored brethren. Oh, I know there is more glamor,
more romance, in the work far away, but the commission is
still: Begin at Jerusalem!

AND SAMARIA

But we are not to stop there. Jesus said, *beginning* at Jerusalem. And so next comes the lad in Samaria, and finally
the Greeks from far away. This was the order Andrew un-
consciously followed. What a day it was when his *own* brother,
Simon, was saved. And then came the lad, and through the
lad five thousand were fed, and finally, the Greeks, and as we
mentioned before, one is traditionally supposed to have been
Dr. Luke, and through him countless millions have been
blessed. The narrative in John 12 gives us a little glimpse
of how Andrew was regarded by these other disciples as a
soul winner. The narrative will bear repeating:

"And there were certain Greeks among them that
came up to worship at the feast:

The same came therefore to Philip, which was of

Bethsaida of Galilee, and desired him, saying, Sir, we would see Jesus" (John 12:20-21).

These Greeks were evidently from Galilee of the Gentiles, for in seeking an interview with Jesus, they came to Philip, evidently because he too was from Bethsaida of Galilee. So they addressed Philip and said: "Sir, we would see Jesus."

And now, follow most carefully the next verse:

"Philip cometh and telleth *Andrew*" (John 12:22).

Why did not Philip answer these Greeks and bring them to Jesus directly? There must be some reason, for instead of taking these Greeks directly to Jesus, he goes instead to Andrew, and tells him, "Here are some Greeks who want to be brought to Christ." And then Andrew and Philip (not Philip and Andrew) but *Andrew* and Philip came and told Jesus. How superbly wonderful and instructive all of this becomes!

Philip seems to say to these Greeks, "You want to meet Jesus? Just a moment. Just wait a minute. I know just the fellow who can do that kind of a job. I know a man who knows how to bring people to Christ better than anyone else. You know, he brought his own brother, Simon, and he brought a little lad once, and what a miracle followed! I'll go and get him," and he fetched Andrew, and Andrew brought them to Jesus.

Andrew had evidently gained a reputation among the disciples for bringing individuals to the Lord Jesus. He was known as a soul winner, a personal worker. He was not known for his oratory, his literary ability, his great personality, his popularity. He could not sway a crowd, but he could persuade one soul for Christ. Oh, beloved, I say this honestly and sincerely, I would rather be known for my ability to kneel with a poor, lost sinner in an obscure corner, or in a gutter, than to be known as the greatest preacher on earth with all of its temptations, pitfalls and added responsibilities which are peculiar to a popular ministry. I would like to have people remember me as the man who knew how to kneel with a sinner in the dust and to win a soul for Christ. I am sure that the greatest rewards are going to go to those obscure, unappreciated, humble servants of the Lord who never knew the footlights and the spotlights, and who never had a write-up in the papers, but plugged along with the talents they possessed, and were found faithful in the end.

We need once more to get our eyes fixed upon the individual, upon each single sinner. The way the Lord is building His Church is still one by one, by the individual, personal contact of those who, like Andrew, have caught the vision. However, today we are living in an age of mass worship. Things just have to be big. This is certainly the supercolossal age of all history. Everything must be big — big in business; big in religion. We worship bigness as though this were an end in itself. If a meeting is big, that is the yardstick by which we measure it. We measure the success of a program by the crowd, the number of people who come forward, the amount of money we are able to throw around and spend. But I am wondering how God looks at all this, and how it will stack up when Jesus comes.

An Illustration

Here is a preacher endowed by God with a wonderful personality, a marvelous voice, a thorough education, a brilliant mind, all of which was not of his own choosing, but God's gift through his parents and his forebears. He has a great church and a wonderful congregation, has a big salary. Mind you, I don't begrudge him these at all. I just state them as facts. He is popular. Everyone praises him, and they shower him with gifts on every hand. His picture appears in the paper, and he is in great demand everywhere.

That man also has a tremendous responsibility, however, for if he wastes his talent by becoming proud, becoming too big and important to kneel with the drunkard in the gutter, lives on the fat of the land, struts and bows to the plaudits of men, and waters down his message to suit the rich deacons, wastes his time in looking over his investments, he has already had his reward. And if he is really saved, he may awaken to find nothing but ashes left at the judgment seat of Christ.

Out there in the hills is quite another picture, however. In an unpainted house lives a little preacher, one of the little Andrews, serving a church of only fifty members. He receives $35.00 a week, drives a rickety Ford. He is not a great orator, his talents are but few, he has no money to amass a good library or to broaden his education by trans-Atlantic flights. Few ever hear of him, and seldom does he receive a compliment or word of encouragement.

Day in and day out, year in and year out, he pleads and plods through the mud to deal with sinners, to visit the dying poverty-stricken woodsman, to help and assist and preach and work. Long hours he spends agonizing for souls, and dies an early death from overwork and undernourishment. He is buried with but a few people at his funeral, but I want to be there when at the judgment seat of Christ the rewards are handed out, and the gold, silver and precious stones come bright and clear through the fire to gleam upon the breast of the Saviour as He beckons this lowly, unheard of, unsung servant, and says, "Come up here, and sit by Me. Well done, thou good and faithful servant; enter thou into the joy of thy Lord."

Chapter Twenty-three

THE LAST WORD FROM PETER

But grow in grace, and in the knowledge of our Lord and Saviour Jesus Christ. To him be. glory both now and for ever. Amen

II Peter 3:18

THESE are the last words of the tempestuous, stormy petrel among the apostolic band. Peter begins this final letter of only three chapters with the words, "Simon Peter." Simon the name of the old man of the flesh, Peter the name of the new man after the Spirit. These two are used in introducing his last words to the Church. At the very close of his stormy career, he makes no claim to perfection, but still sadly admits that Simon was still there, as well as Peter.

The Scriptures tell us little about the last 20 years of Simon Peter's life and ministry. After his last use of the keys in the tenth chapter of Acts, he soon disappears from view, and apparently is limited in his ministry to Jerusalem. Paul tells us of his visit to Antioch a few years later, but nothing of his activities in the meantime. When Peter wrote his first epistle some six years before his death, he presumably was residing in Babylon, but why, and for how long, we do not know, as the Scriptures are utterly silent on these matters.

PETER AT HOME

The Catholic Church holds and teaches that Peter spent the last years of his life in the city of Rome, and there became

177

the first pope. This teaching is based on tradition, but is not recorded in the record of Scripture. According to tradition Peter died by crucifixion, head down, on a cross, because he felt utterly unworthy to die in the same position as his Lord. If this be so, then this was undoubtedly what our Lord Jesus Christ referred to when He said to Peter in John 21:18,

> "Verily, verily, I say unto thee, When thou wast young, thou girdedst thyself, and walkedst whither thou wouldest: but when thou shalt be old, thou shalt stretch forth thy hands, and another shall gird thee, and carry thee whither thou wouldest not.
>
> This spake he, signifying by what death he should glorify God. And when he had spoken this, he saith unto him, Follow me" (John 21:18-19).

It is inferred from this passage that the stretching forth of his hands probably refers to his extended arms when he was tied to the cross of his death, to be carried to the place of execution, and the words, "Follow Me," are interpreted to mean that he was to follow Christ, even in the method and mode of his death. How much truth there is in this tradition, we do not know, but it certainly does make a fitting climax to the life of this interesting apostle. Whatever truth may be found in this interpretation, one thing we do know was that Peter was to die an unusual death. This is clearly inferred in the words of our Lord.

Just before Peter was to die, he wrote this second epistle. Somehow, the Lord had revealed to Peter that he was soon to go home to glory, and this undoubtedly prompted him to write this last letter. How the Lord revealed this to Peter we do not know, but that the Lord did inform him about his home-going is clear from Peter's own record. Maybe Peter had already been condemned to die, and was

aware of the brevity of his stay here upon the earth, and so
he writes:

"Yea, I think it meet, as long as I am in this tabernacle,
to stir you up by putting you in remembrance;

Knowing that shortly I must put off this my tabernacle, even as our Lord Jesus Christ hath shewed me"
(II Peter 1:13-14).

From this passage it is evident that the Lord had revealed unto Peter that he must shortly go from this life
to be with his Lord.

PETER'S LAST CONCERN

Now we are quite interested to know what was the heaviest
on the heart of Peter as he faced this imminent execution.
One would suppose that he would be feeling sorry for himself, bemoaning his sad fate, and seeking sympathy or help
in this dread hour, in the last moments of his life. But you
may search the entire epistle, and you will not find a word
of complaint. There is no moaning, no repining, no regret, no
fear of any kind. He who had once denied his Lord, and
had cringed before the intimidations of a servant girl, now
faces death and execution without a whimper or complaint.
How Peter himself had grown in grace during those years!
What was on his heart as he wrote this epistle is an amazing
revelation of what the grace of God is able to do in the
life of even such unlikely material as the apostle, Simon
Peter. There are a number of things which lie upon the surface.

HIS TESTIMONY TO THE WORD

The first thing of which he reminds us in this closing
letter is not to forget the authority of the Scriptures. He
says:

"Moreover I will endeavour that ye may be able after my decease to have these things always in remembrance." (II Peter 1:15).

We are led to ask, What things is he talking about? The first which he mentions is a warning against adding to the sacred Word of God. He says in II Peter 1:16,

"For we have not followed cunningly devised *fables,* when we made known unto you the power and coming of our Lord Jesus Christ."

Peter warns against adding anything to the Word of God. Traditions, fables, revelations, or visions are not to be added to the completed Book. Do not forget this, Peter seems to say, and then continues:

"That no prophecy of the scripture is of any private interpretation.

For the prophecy came not in old time by the will of man: but holy men of God spake as they were moved by the Holy Ghost" (II Peter 1:20-21).

No Scripture is of any private interpretation, says Peter. The interpretation of the Word of God is the privilege of every born-again, instructed believer, and is not the private privilege of a few, but is for all. This is an important truth, coming from the lips of the Apostle Peter.

FALSE PROPHETS

From the warning against adding anything whatsoever to the Scriptures, Peter now moves on quite logically in chapter 2 to a solemn warning against false teachers, who would pervert the Scriptures by adding to or taking away or wresting it to their own destruction, according to their own ideas.

The third and the last chapter of Peter's final epistle has to do with the return of the Lord. How precious this truth must have been to the Apostle Peter! He had followed his

Lord some thirty years before, because he had believed that He was the Messiah, the King of Israel, that He was going to set up His Kingdom in Jerusalem, and had promised to Peter and the disciples a place of prominence and authority in this Kingdom. But Peter had to learn the disappointing lesson that his Lord was not to set up His Kingdom at this time, but was to be rejected instead, and go to the Cross of Calvary. He had to learn that the Kingdom must be postponed until His Second Coming. How Peter must have longed for that event, when he with the twelve apostles would sit upon twelve thrones, judging the twelve tribes of Israel. How the words must have rung in his ears when the two men on Mount Olivet said:

"This same Jesus, which is taken up from you into heaven, shall so come in like manner as ye have seen him go into heaven" (Acts 1:11).

Now in view of all this he gives his last fervent pleading and exhortation in verses 11 to 14. After having given us a picture of the end of God's dealing with man here upon the earth, and the fact that Christ is coming back again, and that there is an eternity ahead, he says:

"Seeing then that all these things shall be dissolved, what manner of persons ought ye to be in all holy conversation and godliness,

Looking for and hasting unto the coming of the day of God, wherein the heavens being on fire shall be dissolved, and the elements shall melt with fervent heat?

Nevertheless we, according to his promise, look for new heavens and a new earth, wherein dwelleth righteousness.

Wherefore, beloved, seeing that ye look for such things,

be diligent that ye may be found of him in peace, without
spot, and blameless" (II Peter 3:11-14).

The truth of the Second Coming of the Lord Jesus was
precious to the apostle Peter. The more we grow in grace
and in the knowledge of His Word, and of Him, the more
precious also will this truth become to our hearts.

PETER AND PAUL

The best wine is always kept for the last, and the sweetest
thing about Peter is reserved for the end of his closing epistle.
It is his tender and touching reference to Paul, the apostle,
in which he calls him, "our beloved brother, Paul." We
would like to have you note carefully verse 15:

> "And account that the longsuffering of our Lord is
> salvation; even as *our beloved brother Paul* also according
> to the wisdom given unto him hath written unto you.
>
> As also in all his epistles, speaking in them of these
> things; in which are some things hard to be understood,
> which they that are unlearned and unstable wrest, as they
> do also the other scriptures, unto their own destruction"
> (II Peter 3:15-16).

I am so glad that we have this reference to "our beloved
brother Paul" and to know that everything was out of the
way between these two apostles before Peter came to the end
of the road. For Peter had had a few painful experiences with
the apostle Paul. First, you will recall, Peter was set aside
in order to be replaced by Paul. Peter had held the spotlight
for many years after Christ was here upon earth. He
had been the leader of the twelve. To him had been committed the Keys of the Kingdom of Heaven. He had been
the great preacher at Pentecost. Then there came upon the
scene a younger man, a man who was not one of the original
twelve at all, a man who had persecuted the Church. This

man rose to sudden prominence and totally eclipsed Peter for the rest of his life.

I am sure that this was not an easy pill for Peter to swallow. How he reacted at the time, we do not know, but how refreshing to know that before Peter died, he calls him "our beloved brother Paul." Peter had learned to say about Paul what John the Baptist said about the Lord Jesus:

"He must increase, but I must decrease" (John 3:30).

This may seem like a small incident in the life of Peter, but I know how the lesson is needed today. It is not easy for the flesh to take a lower place, to step aside for another after years of prominence and service. To have a younger man come along and be used of God in your place while you must take the humble position is certainly not pleasing to the natural man and to the flesh. But Peter had learned the lesson of humility, and at the close of his life, he reveals absolutely no jealousy, no hurt pride, no resentment, no bitterness, but says, "our beloved brother Paul."

THE PUBLIC REBUKE

There was still another incident which must have been even harder for Peter to take. It is recorded by Paul in Galatians chapter 2. Paul had preached to the Gentiles in Antioch, and many had been saved. When the apostles in Jerusalem heard about it, Peter went up to Antioch to visit Paul, and the Gentile disciples. When Peter saw the grace of God, he cast off all legal restraints and fellowshipped freely with these Gentiles, and ate and drank with them.

Then some of the legalistic, Judaeizing teachers from Jerusalem came up to see what it was all about, and to spy out their liberty. When they approached, Peter became greatly alarmed, and separated himself again from these Gentile believers, and placed himself back under the law, for fear of these legalistic spies. He put himself back under bondage. This incident so irked and incensed Paul, the great apostle of grace, that he took Peter to task. Here is Paul's record of the incident, as given by him in the second chapter of Galatians:

"But when Peter was come to Antioch, I withstood him to the face, because he was to be blamed.

For before that certain came from James, he did eat with the Gentiles: but when they were come, he withdrew and separated himself, fearing them which were of the circumcision.

And the other Jews dissembled likewise with him; insomuch that Barnabas also was carried away with their dissimulation.

But when I saw that they walked not uprightly according to the truth of the gospel, I said unto Peter before them all, If thou, being a Jew, livest after the manner of Gentiles, and not as do the Jews, why compellest thou the Gentiles to live as do the Jews?

We who are Jews by nature, and not sinners of the Gentiles,

Knowing that a man is not justified by the works of the law, but by the faith of Jesus Christ, even we have believed in Jesus Christ that we might be justified by the faith of Christ, and not by the works of the law: for by the works of the law shall no flesh be justified" (Galatians 2:11-16).

Now do not imagine that this was easy for Peter to endure. This was a public rebuke and was made before all the multitude. Peter, the leader of the apostles, the great preacher of Pentecost, senior by many years over Paul, openly taken to task and severely "dressed down" before the crowd by his junior, Paul. Paul does not tell us what Peter's reaction was at the time, or if he answered Paul at all. But from Peter's last words, we do know that all was forgiven and he calls him, "our beloved brother Paul." It must have been humiliating, indeed, but Peter who began as blustering, impetuous, hot-tempered, trigger-fingered Simon, ready to fight at the drop of the handkerchief, had grown in grace. The last picture of him is a sweet, humble, lovable old man who paid tribute to the man who had humbled him, even though it was justified, more than possibly anyone else had ever done. How wonderful the grace of God is illustrated in Peter.

Practical Lesson

So we conclude these thoughts on Simon Peter. Is there any lesson more needed than the lesson Peter teaches us of humility, forgiveness, graciousness, and love? How slow we are to forgive; how bitter we often remain. How long we carry our grudges, and nurse them, and how pride robs us of the blessing God would have us experience. How we nurse our hurts, how we resent correction. Oh, if we only like Peter, could learn the lesson and heed his closing admonition:

"But grow in grace, and in the knowledge of our Lord and Saviour Jesus Christ. To him be glory both now and for ever. Amen" (II Peter 3:18).